THE REMEDY
OF
SOULS

THE REMEDY OF SOULS

OF

SOULS

FROM ACCUSATIONS
HELD BY MUSLIMS
AGAINST THE PROPHET

SHEIKH ELANAYYAL
ABU GROON

To order additional copies of this book, contact:
Xlibris
800-056-3182
www.Xlibrispublishing.co.uk
Orders@Xlibrispublishing.co.uk
754722

Contents

To you and all humanity, to whom Prophet Muhammad is sent as mercy.

To all those who seek love, peace, and happiness.

To those who—due to their innate nature—know what falls in harmony with their souls.

To those who behold Prophet Muhammad (prayers and blessings of Allah (SWT) be upon him), his parents, and his family as the exemplar of humanity—unsurpassed in knowledge, bravery, forbearance, and nobility both in character and form—but find their stance colliding with what appears within traditional teachings.

Preface

Allah (SWT) says, 'Indeed, the religion to Allah is Islam' (3:19). Thus, no prophet arose except that he conveyed the religion of Islam. Moses (AS), therefore, was a Muslim, and those who follow him are Muslims likewise. Jesus (AS) is Muslim, and those who follow him are Muslims similarly.

Allah (SWT) says regarding the followers of Jesus (AS), 'I will make those who follow you above the unbelievers till the Day of Resurrection' (3:55). He (SWT) did not say 'till the arrival of Muhammad (PBUH)', and hence what's required of them is faith in Muhammad (PBUH) even if they remain within their religion. 'So, the people of the Injeel [Bible] should judge by what Allah has revealed therein' (5:47). 'Had they established the Torah and the Injeel [Bible] and that which was revealed unto them from their Lord, they would have certainly enjoyed abundance from above and from underfoot' (5:66).

Muhammad (PBUH) is the first Muslim, as Allah (SWT) says, 'Say (Oh Muhammad): "Indeed my Prayer, my devotions, my living and dying are only for Allah, the Lord of the Worlds. He has no partner. Thus have I been commanded, and I am the first Muslim"' (6:162–3). All messengers (AS) are Muslims, as are those who follow them and accept as true what they came with.

However, those who followed the messengers were not angels and therefore fell into errors regarding the practice of the religion, and their knowledge likewise fell into error. These errors accumulated through the passage of time to the extent that the basis of the religion virtually became non-existent; thus Allah (SWT) sent further messengers in order to preserve the religion.[1]

Consequently, it is erroneous for the followers of Muhammad (PBUH) to monopolise the term Islam and dissociate it from those who submit to previous scriptures from the past. Nor is it appropriate for them to claim infallibility in preserving the religion that the Messenger, Muhammad (PBUH), came with. It is he (PBUH) who said, 'Indeed, you will follow the path of those who came before you,[2] step by step, and if they entered a lizard's hole, so would you.'[3]

The people of Jesus (AS) venerated him extensively to the point of deifying him. Thereafter, the people of Muhammad (PBUH)— those who came to believe—sought to clarify the mistake of those who preceded them (from the followers of Jesus (AS), who deified him) and ended up maintaining the complete opposite presumption. They stripped the Messenger (PBUH) of perfect human qualities and infallibility and attributed to him errors that would expose to death anyone that would attribute these to a scholar or a leader of the Muslims.

The Messenger (PBUH) is beyond infallibility; *infallibility* refers to a follower (of a messenger) who does not err. However, Muhammad is the *musharri*[4] and not a follower of anyone. In fact, he is absolute truth; therefore, his actions epitomise justice, moral excellence, and revelation. Allah (SWT) commands His Messenger (PBUH) to say, 'I only act upon what is revealed to me' (6:50). Thus, there is no scope for passing judgement upon his actions by those who are inferior in rank; and in fact, all of creation is inferior to him (PBUH)!

---

[1]   As all religions from God are one.

[2]   Meaning the Christians and Jews.

[3]   Sahih al-Bukhari.

[4]   The legislator of human beings.

In this work, I clarify several issues that have been attributed to the seal of the prophets (PBUH) that are unbefitting for even an ordinary believer, let alone for the greatest of God's creation in form, character, knowledge, and perfection, incomparable to anyone from humanity.

Indeed, the prophets of Allah (SWT) merit holiness and reverence, and even if this is denied, it cannot be said that they are other than the foremost in intellect, which is what qualifies them to fulfil the message. If what is found in the sources diminishes the status of any of the prophets, it necessitates scrutiny and verification of its soundness in light of the above and what is mentioned in the revealed Book[5] of Allah (SWT).

Thus, I have reviewed what is found in the Islamic sources in consideration of this understanding. With this review, I hope that I have removed what is attributed to the noble essence of our Prophet (PBUH) and shown that many Muslims have harmed themselves by making accusations that are unbecoming to his elevated status—accusations which have hindered many of our co-religionists from comprehending the greatness of his noble essence.

The greatness and character of Muhammad (PBUH) surpasses Gabriel and the angels, who do not abate in their sending of prayers upon him nor the one who created him—since he is absolute truth. The intellect is befuddled in the comprehension of his greatness. Allah (SWT) says, 'How can Allah guide people who disbelieved after having faith, and affirmed that the Messenger is truth?' (3:86). Allah (SWT) and His angels send blessings upon Muhammad (PBUH). Moreover, He (SWT) sends multifold blessings upon those who send blessings upon Muhammad (PBUH).

---

[5]   Qur'an.

Acknowledgements

I would like to thank Mr Bilal Ali and Dr Abdalla Yassin, OBE, for initiating the translation of the Arabic version of the book and for their efforts in the editing process. I am also grateful to the Onyx Link Foundation for their contribution in publishing this book. Above all, I thank God, the merciful, for enabling me to attempt— through this text—to illustrate the honoured reality of His Messenger, Muhammad (PBUH), as revealed in His book, and to expose some of the falsehoods attributed to him within the Islamic tradition so that it becomes a 'remedy of souls' for Muslims and others through avoiding and rejecting such inequities.

بِسْمِ اللَّهِ الرَّحْمَـٰنِ الرَّحِيمِ

In the name of Allah, the most gracious, the most merciful.

يَا أَيُّهَا الَّذِينَ آمَنُوا اتَّقُوا اللَّهَ وَآمِنُوا بِرَسُولِهِ...

Oh you who came to believe,[1] be conscious of Allah[2] and have true faith in His Messenger.[3]

57:28

يَا أَيُّهَا الَّذِينَ آمَنُوا إِذَا تَنَاجَيْتُمْ فَلَا تَتَنَاجَوْا بِالْإِثْمِ وَالْعُدْوَانِ وَمَعْصِيَتِ الرَّسُولِ...

Oh you who came to believe, when you converse, do not talk of sin, transgression, and disobedience to the Messenger.

58:09

كَيْفَ يَهْدِي اللَّهُ قَوْمًا كَفَرُوا بَعْدَ إِيمَانِهِمْ وَشَهِدُوا أَنَّ الرَّسُولَ حَقٌّ...

How would Allah bestow His guidance upon people who have resolved to deny the truth after they had attained faith in it, and after having borne witness that the Messenger is the truth.

03:86

---

[1]   Generic name given to the people to whom Prophet Muhammad (PBUH) is sent.

[2]   The name for God Almighty in the Arabic language.

[3]   The translation we have referred to are well known English translations—such as Yusuf Ali, Marmaduke Pickthall, A. J. Arberry—but our version is based on the Arabic of the Qur'an.

Our Vision

To those who seek truth and safety in the hereafter; to those who have become exhausted from the complications of *knowledge*, the disagreements of the schools of thought and jurisprudence, and the clash of religious texts; to those who are overcome by the confusion abundant in the collections of differing religious writings, narrations, history, and *ahadith*;[1] to those who have endeavoured with all their hearts in search of truth in order to achieve salvation against the tide of distorted paths that lead to nowhere or of traces that lead to a pit of fire; to those who—due to their pure nature—know what falls in harmony with their souls but find it colliding with what appears within traditional teachings; to those who behold the Messenger of God (PBUH)[2] as the exemplar of humanity—unsurpassed in knowledge, bravery, forbearance, and nobility both in character and form—to the extent that the intellect stumbles in setting forth his perfect ever-existent character, which none can set forth or reach, thus making all descriptions fall short; to the lovers of the Prophet (PBUH) who do not need to be told that he is not reachable to all of creation in his essence, his knowledge, his character, and his form; to these I put forth a balance, and through its observance, it is hoped that one's consideration of his Beloved will rest safe, and the soundness of faith in him will be attained.

---

[1]   The plural of Hadith, sayings of the Prophet (PBUH).

[2]   A short form of 'Peace and blessings of Allah (SWT) be upon him, his parents, and his family'.

Allah (SWT)[3] declares, 'Verily, in the Messenger of Allah you have an excellent example [to follow] for the one who looks forward [with hope and awe] to Allah and the Last Day' (33:21); this signifies perfection of conduct and human morality. Thus conduct that emanates from the Prophet (PBUH) is nothing less than perfect, imperative to pattern, as there exists none more virtuous. Whoever deems that the possibility exists for the Prophet's conduct and behaviour to be surpassed by another from creation, such a person has ruined his worldly and other-worldly life. By deeming another to exceed the Prophet (PBUH), one diminishes his status, contradicts the Qur'anic text, and adopts another as the standard of reference.[4]

Thus, conduct that you (oh reader) would refuse to accept for yourself you must restrain from attributing to the beloved (PBUH) since he is your standard of reference. It is unbelievable that the conduct of the standard that one is obliged to follow will be that which one will not even attribute to oneself, let alone to one's parents, and hence under no circumstances can the likes be attributed to the beloved (PBUH). Moreover, conduct that you find reprehensible to attribute to your teachers, sheikhs, or spiritual guides you must fully reject ascribing it to the beloved since he is the greatest teacher (PBUH).

Any attribute that Allah (SWT) ascribes to a disbeliever or condemns a sinner with must be denied for the beloved (PBUH). And thus if Allah (SWT) describes a disbeliever with His words 'Then he frowned and scowled' (74:22), frowning becomes a reprehensible attribute of the character of the disbeliever since Allah (SWT) has used it to condemn as such. Consequently, it becomes mandatory to elevate the beloved (PBUH) far above such a characteristic, and it is unfitting for us believers who love the beloved to harbour doubts about whom 'He frowned, turned away and left' (80:1) was revealed if we refuse the statements of the *mufassirun*[5]—who claim that it was revealed

---

3   A short form of the Arabic 'Subhanahu wa Ta'ala,' meaning 'Glory be to him the Most High.'

4   The standard of reference or criterion of the truth for reverting one's entire affairs towards.

5   Interpreters of the Qur'an.

in respect to the Prophet (PBUH)—since the mufassirun are not infallible.

Moreover, the instances of lapses of historians and distortions of history itself are matters that people of intellect cannot disregard. The influence of political systems upon culture by past regimes and the likelihood of insertions upon tradition on the part of enemies—those envious and those of opposing hostile thought—are consequences that no book can be exempt from.[6]

Allah (SWT) has obligated us through the glorious Qur'an to deem the Prophet (PBUH) elevated due to the great Muhammadan character, upon which He took an oath in Surah Qalam: '[By] Noon[7] and the Pen, and what they write' (68:01); therefore, no consideration should be given to the sayings of those who attribute to the beloved (PBUH) reprehensible character, which Allah (SWT) uses to describe a cursed disbeliever! Moreover, why do we attribute infallibility to the mufassirun and the collectors of Hadith in all that they say and write to the extent of accepting everything that comes from them even if it's contesting the infallibility of the Prophet (PBUH)? Is not the other way around, which is the truth, the appropriate position? Should we not reserve infallibility for the Prophet (PBUH) in all he said and did; contest what they say about him; and reject all that present a portrayal of deficiency in his perfect character and form?

Allah (SWT) says, 'And indeed, you are of the most exalted integrity of morals' (68:4). The beloved (PBUH) mentions this regarding himself: 'Verily, I have been sent to perfect moral character.'[8] This is the foundation and criterion: denial of all that is contrary is critical and a religious duty upon all Muslims, and holding on to a conviction other than this is abandoning the (true) religion.

For he who claims that the will of Allah (SWT) was to teach His Prophet or discipline him has indeed stationed himself upon that

---

6   Except the Qur'an itself.
7   *Noon* is a letter of the Arabic alphabet.
8   Musnad Ahmad.

which is inadmissible. The will of Allah (SWT) is out of bounds for him; he can neither elucidate nor express it, and as such has no right to claim 'Allah (SWT) willed . . ." by utilising independent reasoning (*ijtihad*)[9] through his intellect without recourse to textual proof. This is akin to laying claim to prophethood.

Moreover, the Prophet (PBUH) said, 'I was sent as a teacher.'[10] So the provision of knowledge of the Messenger (PBUH) from Allah (SWT), if not before the message, must be with and not after it in order for him to bestow his knowledge upon people to teach them. It is beyond the Messenger (PBUH) that he would require teaching from them or learn in their midst when he had been sent to them.

Allah (SWT) says, 'He it is Who has sent to the Ummys[11] a Messenger from among themselves, one who recites to them His verses, purifies them, and teaches them the Book and the Wisdom, although before this they were in manifest error' (62:02); so he is not to be deemed inferior to nor similar to any one of them. The Prophet (PBUH) said, 'Indeed, I am unlike any one of you.'[12] As for his discipline, it is unbefitting for Allah (SWT) to send him before disciplining him (PBUH) or to delay it so as to complete it in front of the very people he was sent, showing them his lack of discipline or the deficiency in his knowledge in order to embarrass or harm him.

Or perhaps the Messenger (PBUH), whom He has sent, is still in need of human perfection, which qualifies him for being a messenger. And why? Does this position increase their certainty in this statement of the Messenger (PBUH): 'I was sent as a teacher'?[13] Or is it doubting this statement or rather rejecting it outright? Does his appearance with such deficiencies in knowledge and character give solid evidence that he indeed was sent by Allah (SWT) in order for people to accept

---

[9]   *Ijtihad* is an Islamic legal term that means 'independent reasoning' or 'the utmost effort an individual can put forth in an activity'.

[10] Sunan ibn Majah.

[11] Those who had not received scripture previously.

[12] Musnad Ahmad.

[13] Sunan ibn Majah.

Islam? And how on earth can his need for discipline be reconciled with his statement 'My Lord instilled adab [discipline] within me, and refined my upbringing with beautiful adab'?[14] Can it be that his appearance with such deficiencies in character or knowledge was necessary in order for us to have faith in him as the Messenger sent by God? This would suggest that Allah (SWT) did not send His beloved perfect in character and fully competent to be obeyed by His permission whilst He says: 'And We have not sent forth a Messenger but [for him] to be obeyed in accordance with the Will of Allah' (4:64).

Indeed, some Muslims have taken the position that it is possible to be in opposition to the Prophet (PBUH) despite this noble verse and won't lay blame upon anyone who does so (i.e. one who opposes the Messenger). Moreover, some have gone to the extent of believing that the truth is with such a person! As a result, this opposer becomes the one obeyed by the will of God!

---

14   Fuaad al-Majmuah.

Introduction

All praise is due to Allah (SWT), who brought the worlds into being by the light of His manifestations. And He fashioned their alignment of harmony in the perfect form with beauty and refinement. He raised the heavens without pillars, furnished them with constellations, beautified them with celestial bodies, and established the balance.[1] He blessed the earth, ordained therein all the worldly means of sustenance, and granted vicegerency[2] to the human being.

I bear witness that there is none worthy of worship except Allah (SWT) alone. He is one and has no partners, the bestower of compassion and bounties, the one who made the darkness and light for distinction.

He did not abandon the human being; he clarified for him the path of truth and of failure. Thus, He sent His messengers as bearers of glad tidings and heralds throughout history. He concluded and sealed them with the best of His messengers, Muhammad, the son of Adnan,[3] whom He exalted, ennobled, made beloved, and granted with intercession in the hereafter. And He and His angels showered their prayers and blessings upon him and commanded the people of faith to do likewise.

---

[1] Balance of nature for natural reactions and that of morality for human interaction.

[2] Khilafah.

[3] An ancestor of the Prophet (PBUH).

Oh, Allah (SWT), send prayers and blessings upon him and his family and allow this prayer to include us amongst his beloveds and allow us to serve at his side. Enable us to expose falsehood and avoid it and to clearly illustrate his honoured reality as you have revealed in your book and to demonstrate that he has no partner in the fulfilment of the message entrusted to him nor is there a prophet after him.

In the name of Allah (SWT), we begin.

The one whom Allah (SWT) has chosen to deliver His message will never be but the supreme example of its understanding and practice; hence, the perfection of acting upon it cannot be seen except through him. And whatsoever is obscured from the message is not clarified except through the Chosen One's[4] actions or words. It is inconceivable that another could be more knowledgeable than him of any small or great matter of his message. Therefore, no interpretation of what the Messenger (PBUH) has been sent with should be taken from another in his time. Moreover, no one has the right to interpret or clarify the Holy Qur'an in the Messenger's auspicious presence or to accuse him of inaccuracy in relation to his Lord.

To hold a position other than this is to accuse the Messenger (PBUH) of deficiency regarding the fulfilment of his message due to ignorance or to an error in conduct on his part. This would imply that he is not the standard reference[5] concerning what he was sent with! Such a position, in fact, resembles the statement of those who claim, 'You are not a Messenger' (13:43). This claim causes the relationship between the Messenger (PBUH) and the one who sent him to be lost since this is the criterion for such a reference.

As for those who claim a better understanding and practice of the message than the Messenger (PBUH), there is nothing that could

---

4　　The Messenger is also known as the Chosen One (Mustafa).

5　　The standard reference of Islam (i.e. he is the source of the truth), as Allah (SWT) says, 'And whatever the Messenger consigns unto you, take it, and from whatever he forbids you, abstain' (59:7). This entails that no believer should disagree with him or disobey him.

support the soundness of their claim except if they were a co-partner in delivering the message, in which case the claimant would be able to rely upon the same source as the Messenger (PBUH). And this is impossible. Allah (SWT) chose His honoured Messenger (PBUH) and preferred Him above all others; no associate does he have in delivering the message, nor is there anyone superior to him! He has no parallel amongst humankind, much less someone who can correct him regarding what he was sent with. In fact, Allah (SWT) assigned to him the entire affair, saying, '[O Muhammad], they should not contest with you concerning this affair, and call them to Your Lord. You are certainly on the Straight Path' (22:67).

Therefore, it is impossible for anyone who contests with the Messenger (PBUH) to rely upon the one who sent him[6] or on the message itself to justify his claims without being an associate in messengership, which is inconceivable. This position would surely indicate doubt regarding the Messenger's connection with Allah (SWT) and imply that he is not the most preferred by Allah (SWT) in undertaking this mission. More seriously, it doubts the choice of Allah (SWT) in choosing the best to fulfil His message!

In the same vein—after having faith—the contesting individual is required by the one who sent the Messenger (PBUH) to follow him upon his footsteps and not to contest, as contesting renders one's deeds fruitless even by merely raising the voice.[7] Thus, faith in the Messenger (PBUH), acceptance of his every speech and action, and total surrender to him are the demands of Allah (SWT) for His believing servants. Allah (SWT) said, 'O Believers, obey Allah and obey the Messenger and do not cause your deeds to be rendered fruitless' (47:33). Allah (SWT) also said, 'O believers, be heedful of Allah and have faith in His Messenger' (57:28).

It is the Messenger (PBUH) who brings out those who believe and do righteous deeds from the recesses of darkness into the light. Allah (SWT) says, 'A Messenger who recites to you the clear verses of Allah,

---

6   Allah (SWT).

7   See verse 49:2.

so that he [the Messenger] may bring out those who believe and do righteous deeds, from the recesses of darkness to the light' (65:11). The Messenger (PBUH) is peerless in his knowledge, his intellect, his virtue, and his perfect moral qualities, for he is the noblest of Allah's creations and the most honourable of them.

Based on this, there is no possibility for comparing action or speech of the Prophet (PBUH) with another to determine which is superior! It is not possible for anyone to be on equal footing or close in deed, speech, perfection of form, character, or knowledge to the one who is chosen by Allah (SWT) to fulfil His message; therefore, there is no scope for comparison to begin with. Any doubtful report in the Islamic tradition that is found inconsistent with this necessitates scrutiny, research, and verification so as to identify corrupt insertions and ill will—thereby invalidating it—and avoid the resulting damnation of whoever accepts such allegations against the exalted status of the Prophet (PBUH).

Nor is it acceptable to turn a blind eye with the pretext of 'This is what our predecessors were upon.' Not everything that the predecessors were upon was praiseworthy. If they were free of mistakes, people would not need messengers to be sent to them one after the other. To sanctify all that the predecessors were upon—conceding to them infallibility, forbidding criticism of them, and rejecting any correction of their errors—is a total vacation of reason. Furthermore, it limits the blessings of Allah (SWT) to them alone. Who was it that delivered the fatwa[8] that the blessings and favours of Allah (SWT) came to an end at the time of the predecessors and have now become barren? No significance is to be given to what the predecessors were upon if it contradicts the book of Allah (SWT) and the *ismah*[9] of the prophets; may His blessings be upon them. Understanding is not sacred, and the predecessors were not infallible.

---

[8]   Legal opinion.

[9]   The ismah of the Prophet (PBUH) stems from the fact that he is haqq (03:86; 17:105): 'absolute truth'. This means that whatever he has said, done, or approved of was not just absolutely right but law, precedence, and illustration of perfection, 'Verily, in the Messenger of God Almighty you have a good example (to follow)' (33:21).

However, some people may consider this proposition to be a deviation from and destruction of their foundations and principles, which are based upon the understanding and the legal verdicts of those who came before them; Allah (SWT) says, 'And when it is said unto them: "Come to what Allah has revealed, and come to the Messenger," they say: "The way of our forefathers suffices us"' (5:104). It's as if the passage of time had bestowed upon the predecessors a type of sanctity and infallibility!

Fanaticism is the great disease and mortal enemy of freedom of thought that the Prophet of mercy (PBUH) invited us towards and that Allah (SWT) revealed in His scripture. Fanaticism also leads to violence and not to the aim of all the divine messages—peace. Informing the human being of Allah (SWT) is the foundation. 'And We have not sent before you a Messenger except that we revealed to him: "There is no God but Me, so get to know Me"'[10] (21:25). Hence the Prophet (PBUH), during his conquest of Makkah, did not enforce Islam upon its inhabitants, nor did he force upon them *jizyah*.[11] Rather, he left them free (to think and believe as they wished); whoever wishes to, let him believe, and whoever wishes not to, let him disbelieve.[12]

Among those who were present and listening to him (PBUH) were Abu Sofian and his son Muawiyah; thus, none can say that whoever was present and listening to the words of the Prophet (PBUH) at the time pronounced the testimony of faith and became companions! Nor did the Prophet (PBUH) put anyone to death during the conquest of Makkah. On the contrary, he absolved himself of the actions of Khalid bin Waleed,[13] who killed some of the non-Muslims of Makkah by stating: 'O Allah (SWT), I am free from what Khalid has done.' The Prophet (PBUH) even refused to invoke against the polytheists

---

[10] 'Worship me' was explained by Ibn Abbas (the cousin of the Prophet (PBUH)) as 'Get to know me'.

[11] Exemption tax taken from non-Muslim citizens (Ahlu al-Dhimmah).

[12] See verse 20:29.

[13] A *sahabi* (companion) who killed a group of people during the conquest of Makkah.

when he was asked by his companions to do so, responding; 'I was not sent to curse, indeed I was sent as a mercy.'[14]

From this juncture, it is imperative to re-examine what we find our predecessors attributed to the noble person of the Prophet (PBUH) and the accusations made against him. The reference source of the truth for this will be what Allah (SWT) revealed and the person of the noble Prophet (PBUH) himself that Allah (SWT) preferred above not only those present during his time but for all times. Allah (SWT) praised him as the possessor of perfect moral character and described him as the mercy for all creation, and he sent him to teach humanity His revelation and wisdom. Thus, there are no actions more beautiful than his, no words more proficient than his, and no essence more virtuous than his. He is peerless in form, attributes, and knowledge. May peace and blessings be upon him, the ennobled beloved, his parents, and his family.

Undeniably, the sources of Islam contain within them accusations against the person of the Messenger of Allah (PBUH), and it is not possible to remain silent about them. Indeed, the danger of keeping silent about them has made it mandatory for me to expose them, clarify them, and confront anyone who believes in them by making apparent the real truth and the profound evidence in the book of Allah (SWT).

Thus, it may be a reminder for anyone who has heard of these accusations and accepted them heedlessly and an enlightenment for anyone who adopts them just as he adopts one of the matters of the religion from his teacher, presuming it an obligation to be taken as it is without critical thinking and justifying his acceptance by the pretext that they exist in the canonical sources of Islam. May it also be an invitation to anyone who, due to these accusations, has left the religion of Islam. Upon Allah (SWT) is the guidance to the right path!

---

[14]   Sahih al-Bukhari.

1

The Accusation of Frowning in the Face of the Blind Man

Before the beginning of time, divine will—emanating from divine knowledge, the goal of the eternal life—has already come to pass through displaying its magnificent zenith in form and character. Thus, omnipotence shone upon the realm of existence by manifesting the perpetually beloved, Muhammad, the son of Abdullah. And He and His angels prayed upon him before his emergence into the physical domain, before the onset of time! And what is time to humanity except night and day, resulting from the movement of celestial bodies? And yet not the essence of time: 'It is not in the nature of the sun to outreach the moon, nor does the night overtake the day, but all in their orbits, are flowing in harmony' (36:40).

Allah (SWT) loved, honoured, prayed upon him (PBUH), bestowed virtues upon him until he was satisfied, and praised him with the eternal words 'And indeed, you are upon a great integrity of morals' (64:4). Hence, his nature upon which he was created was by necessity devoid of harshness, as that would otherwise contradict the divine praise for him. And Allah (SWT) confirmed this truth by saying, 'By Mercy from Allah you (O Muhammad) were lenient towards them. And had you been harsh or hard-hearted, they would have abandoned you' (3:159). And if there emerged a necessity for harshness due to a

1

certain situation, then Allah (SWT) would command him thus: 'Oh Prophet, strive hard against the deniers of the truth and the hypocrites, and be harsh with them' (9:73). *Striving (jihad)* in this context doesn't mean fighting, since hypocrites are apparently in line with Muslims, but they conceal disbelief.

It is said that a blind man approached the one who was created devoid of harshness and praised by his boundless Creator with great, noble character to ask him about that which he was sent with—moral character (as he affirmed, 'Verily, I was only sent to perfect moral character').[1] There was with him at the time a person from amongst the disbelievers; it is said that it was either Ubay bin Khalaf[2] or Utbah bin Rabiah.[3]

The Prophet (PBUH) intended for this disbeliever to be purified with Islam and be taken out from the darkness of *shirk*.[4] However, nothing emanated from him (PBUH) except the predisposition to incline with his whole being towards the blind man that had approached him out of reverence of Allah (SWT). This shows the perfect moral character he was sent with in harmony with the praise of Allah (SWT). It is inconceivable to ascribe to him other than this in the delivering of his message. It is far from the Messenger of Allah (PBUH) that he would frown in the face of a blind man unable to see or ignore him by being preoccupied with the disbeliever who hadn't yet embraced Islam: 'No! Indeed, these verses are a reminder' (80:11).

In fact, there is no liability upon the Messenger (PBUH), except to deliver the message, to be eager in guiding those whom he conveys the message to. Allah (SWT) says, 'If you should be eager for their guidance, indeed, Allah does not bestow His guidance upon any whom He judges to have gone astray' (16:37). Thus, it was the disbeliever who became angry, frowned in the face of the Prophet

---

[1]   Musnad Ahmed.

[2]   A non-Muslim who was a contemporary and an enemy of Muhammad (PBUH).

[3]   A prominent leader of Quraish during the era of Muhammad (PBUH).

[4]   Polytheism.

(PBUH), and turned away, as had occurred earlier with his associate in disbelief.[5] Allah (SWT) described it thus: 'He frowned and scowled; then he turned back displaying his arrogance' (74:22–23). Frowning and turning away from the truth are attributes of disbelievers.

Following the arrival of the blind man, the disbeliever (Allah's imprecation be upon him) arose and turned away from having audience with the Messenger (PBUH). He left, feeling not in need of the Prophet, who prefers a blind man over him. Yet the Prophet (PBUH) was still tending towards him to take him out of the darkness of shirk and purify him with the light of Islam.

Allah (SWT) would not leave the behaviour displayed by the disbeliever in the presence of His beloved without reprimand and condemnation and thus said 'He [the disbeliever] frowned, turned away, and left' (80:1) when the blind companion approached the Messenger (PBUH) 'because the blind man came to him [interrupting]' (80:2). The divine speech is then aimed directly towards the disbeliever, making evident to him his ignorance and showing him that the blind man desired purification: 'And what would make you see [O disbeliever], that perhaps he [the blind man] might be purified or seek knowledge and the knowledge would benefit him?' (80:3,4). Thereupon, the divine speech is affectionately directed towards the Prophet (PBUH): 'As for he [the disbeliever] who thinks himself to be self-sufficient, to him you still give attention' (80:5, 6). That is to say, 'how noble your character and vast your forbearance that you yet turn towards such a one who deems himself self- sufficient, having concern for him? This is solely because you are the gift of mercy.' As Allah (SWT) says, 'And We have not sent you (O Muhammad) but as mercy to all creation' (21:106), not simply Muslims!

This signifies the comprehensive mercy that encompasses disbelievers, jinn, and all of creation. May prayers and blessings of Allah (SWT) be upon you, the all-embracing mercy of Allah (SWT)! Thus,

---

5   Walid bin Almughirah, the chief of the Banu Makhzum clan of the Quraish tribe.

Allah (SWT) intimates for the messenger (PBUH) not to burden or concern himself regarding the turning away of the disbeliever and the disbeliever's arrogance. 'There is (no blame) upon you, if he [the disbeliever] will not be purified' (80:7) since all that is required of the messenger (PBUH) is to deliver the message and not to burden himself more than this.

Further, Allah (SWT) says, 'We have not sent down to you the Qur'an to be a cause of distress to you' (20:20); 'Then perhaps you [O Muhammad] would torment yourself through grief and sorrow over them if they do not believe in this message' (18:6); 'Indeed, Allah misguides whom He wills and guides whom He wills. So do not press yourself to sorrow over them' (35:8); and finally, 'No responsibility is upon the Messenger, except to deliver [the message]' (5:99).

Thereafter, Allah (SWT) praises His Prophet (PBUH) for his concern regarding the blind man and for not ignoring him since he came with earnest purpose. In fact, the conduct of the Prophet (PBUH) was opposite to that of the disbeliever. It was the disbeliever who 'frowned, turned away and left' and abandoned the Prophet (PBUH), the noblest, most honourable creation of Allah (SWT). As for the Prophet (PBUH), he attended to the poor blind man and did not neglect him. 'As for the one who came to you with earnest purpose, in awe of (Allah); you would renounce him? Never' (80:8–11). This conduct is not from the temperament that he was predisposed with. 'Indeed, these verses are a reminder; so whoever wills may remember it' (80:11–12).

Allah (SWT) says, 'No responsibility is upon the Messenger, except to deliver (the message). And Allah knows what you reveal and what you conceal' (5:99).

Let us consider what is mentioned in the *tafsir*[6] of al-Tabari, which contradicts what is mentioned above and typifies the hundreds of *tafasir*[7] that accept as true the attribution of frowning in the face of

---

6   An exegesis of the Qur'an.
7   Plural of *tafsir*.

the blind man to the beloved (PBUH). Moreover, one will find in the tafasir, which has been translated into multiple languages, all the evidence for those people to support their insult of the great Messenger due to ignorance or heedlessness of the actual interpretation.

Al-Tabari says:

> Ibn Umm Makhtum approached, while the Prophet (PBUH) was occupied with one of the dignitaries of Quraish, inviting him to Allah (SWT). The Prophet (PBUH) had a strong desire that they [the dignitaries of Quraish] would become Muslim, since their accepting Islam would mean the Islam of those under their influence. Meanwhile, Ibn Um Makhtum, the blind man, approached, and said; 'Oh messenger of God, teach me from what Allah (SWT) has taught you'; and made his request repeatedly, not knowing he was busy with someone other than himself. This continued until aversion appeared upon the face of the messenger (PBUH) due to the interruption, saying to himself, 'these people [the Quraish], will say: the people who follow him are only the blind, the downtrodden and the slaves', thereupon, he frowned and turned away from him [the blind man], and so the verse was revealed.[8]

Frowning is an attribute of disbelievers, as Allah (SWT) says, depicting a disbeliever, 'Then he frowned and scowled' (74:22). It is altogether appropriate that it be attributed to the disbeliever who was being invited to Islam by the Prophet (PBUH). When he realised that the Prophet (PBUH) diverted his attention to the blind man that had approached, he (the disbeliever) frowned and turned away. If one were to attribute 'frowning' to the Prophet (PBUH), it would entail ascribing him a behaviour contrary to his purpose. Regarding the aim of his message, the Prophet (PBUH) said, 'Indeed, I have only been sent to perfect moral character.'[9]

---

[8]   Tafsir al-Tabari.
[9]   Musnad Ahmad.

Moreover, attributing 'frowning' to the Messenger (PBUH) is in total conflict to the praise of Allah (SWT) for His noblest creation: 'And indeed, you are of the most exalted integrity of morals' (68:4). Yet the mufassirun,[10] in interpreting these verses, have adopted a path of fabricating a story that never was by stating, 'Until aversion appeared upon the face of the messenger (PBUH).' They have no evidence for this! Who was the one who testified to them that he saw this aversion upon the face of the messenger (PBUH)? Was this the blind man or the disbeliever? Or perhaps this *mufassir*[11] was present at the scene? Moreover, they add, 'Saying to himself . . .' Who claims to be aware of what lies in the heart of the Prophet (PBUH) other than Allah (SWT)? Those who assert to this knowledge are making claim to divinity and knowledge of the unseen!

What exacerbates this claim is this statement of theirs: 'The Prophet (PBUH) had a strong desire that they (the dignitaries of Quraish) would become Muslim.' It is far from the Messenger of Allah (PBUH) to act in conflict with what he was sent with. Allah (SWT) says, 'There is not upon the Messenger except the (responsibility for) delivering the message' (24:54). Further clarifying, Allah (SWT) says, 'Not upon you (O Muhammad), is [responsibility for] their guidance' (2:272). Thus, the fabrication 'The Prophet (PBUH) had a strong desire that they [the dignitaries of Quraish] would become Muslim' is nothing less than a claim to knowledge of what lies hidden in the hearts—knowledge reserved for Allah (SWT) alone.

Yet with this false claim, they attributed to the messenger of Allah a contradiction of what is revealed to him in his heart since 'there is not upon the Messenger except the [responsibility for] delivering the message' (24:54). This is the outline of calling to the way of Allah (SWT). Moreover, they employed a falsehood in accusing the messenger (PBUH): 'Saying to himself, "these people [the Quraish] will say: the people who follow him are only the blind, the downtrodden and the slaves."' They attribute to him the worst of what a person may describe his companions as. This is nothing but

---

10   Qur'anic interpreters.

11   Qur'anic interpreter.

fabrication that no one knows how they came up with, yet they dare to attribute it to Allah (SWT) and His Prophet (PBUH)! Allah (SWT) says, 'And that was their falsehood and what they were fabricating' (46:26).

al-Qurtubi, in his tafsir, states, 'Al-Abs [frowning] has a qualified etymology, Abasa, Ya'basu Abusan.[12] Al-Abs, also means that which is smeared on the tails of camels, of urine and dung.'[13] It is also mentioned that Ibn Um Makhtum resided in Medina, and used to call the azan[14] before Bilal (RA)[15] for the morning prayer, whilst Sura Abasa is Makkan[16] according to consensus. If this is the case, then there is no basis for the Hadith that is mentioned in relation to the chapter 'Abasa', such as the Hadith that states: 'Welcome to the one for whom my Lord reprimanded me.' Nor is there for all that is said which attributes frowning to the messenger of Allah (PBUH). It is also reported that Ibn Umm Makhtum was the bearer of the black flag in the Battle of Qadisiyyah.[17] Was his sight restored subsequently, and when?

Ibn Katheer says, 'According to Anas ibn Malik, who said: "I saw him on the day of Qadisiyyah covered in armour, grasping on to a black flag (i.e. Ibn Umm Makhtum)."'[18]

It is also acknowledged that the one to whom the Prophet (PBUH) was advocating Islam when Ibn Umm Makhtum appeared was either Utbah bin Rabiah or Ubay ibn Khalaf, both of whom were from the people of Makkah. Consequently, the incident must've occurred in

---

[12] Arabic words are in the majority derived from root letters.

[13] Tafseer al-Qurtubi.

[14] Call to prayer.

[15] A phrase meaning 'May God be pleased with him'.

[16] The chapters of the Qur'an are classified as being revealed in Makkah or Medina.

[17] Engagement between the Sasanian Empire and the Muslims.

[18] Tafsir Ibn Kathir.

Makkah, yet Ibn Umm Makhtum resided in Medina since he was the *muaddhin*[19] of the Prophet (PBUH) in the city.

Hence, many of these transmitted tafasir make claims regarding the beloved of Allah (SWT) that he acted in contradiction to what he was sent with—as if, despite the fact that he was sent to perfect moral character, he reacted with ill character and frowned in the face and turned away from one who asked him about his very purpose. In other words, he contravened his Lord and his message and acted contrary to what he was sent with! This is how their interpretations depict the character of the Messenger that Allah (SWT) praised, attributing to him the character of the disbeliever whom Allah (SWT) cursed in His statement 'Then he frowned and scowled' (74:22).

Is this how the messenger of Allah (PBUH) is depicted—as one who would frown in the face of poor people and exude ill character so that his error becomes fundamental in delivering the message? Acting contrary to the purpose of his mission necessarily negates his obedience to Allah (SWT), who established that obedience to the Messenger is obedience to Allah. Moreover, it would point the praise of Allah (SWT) for him as being misplaced! And the advocates of this error provide justification for those who oppose the messenger (PBUH)—as though he contravened Allah (SWT) in conveying the message—regardless of Allah (SWT) saying 'Let those who contravene the Prophet's order be warned' and 'Whatever the Messenger consigns unto you, take it, and whatever he forbids you from, abstain' (59:7).

---

19   Caller to prayer.

2

The Accusation of the Devil
Interjecting upon His Tongue

Allah (SWT) has not created such beauty since the beginning of existence, nor has He fashioned the likes of him in equivalence; the most beautiful creation without exception. Imam al-Ghazzali (RH)[1] mentions, 'To have creation superior than the zenith of perfection is beyond the realms of possibility.' Muhammad (blessings and peace be upon him, his parents and his family) was so perfect to the extent that someone in splendid poetry about him said:

> My eyes have gazed upon none more beautiful, And women
> have given birth to none more honourable, You were
> fashioned faultless, as if created in your preference.[2]

He achieved the purpose of beauty in character that was the source of praise by the one who fashioned him out of love for his noble essence and revealed, 'And indeed, you are of the most exalted integrity of morals' (68:4), to be recited throughout the ages. And out of love for him, He became the Disposer of all his actions. 'It was not you who

---

[1]   *Rahimahu Allah*: 'God's mercy be upon him'.

[2]   This poem has been traditionally attributed to Hasan Bin Thabit, a companion of the Prophet (PBUH)

threw [the sand, Oh Prophet], when you threw, but it was Allah who
threw' (8:17). And out of the greatness of His love for him, He said
to him, 'The concern of all matters is not yours (but that of Allah's)'
(3:128). So the Disposer becomes the one who acts on his behalf.

Therefore, whatever he intends to do, his Disposer (glory be to Him)
fulfils it. Furthermore, what he intends in fact is what Allah intends
and enacts. He and His angels sent prayers upon him, unlike any
of the prophets before him, and indeed He sends prayers manifold
upon those who send prayers upon him. Furthermore, He (SWT)
commanded the believers to send prayers upon him. Those who
disregard this command place themselves on the side of the one[3] who
was commanded before to prostrate himself to His slave[4] but refused
and was exiled from His mercy till the Day of Judgement. And He
cautioned those who contravene him, 'Let those who contravene the
Prophet's order be warned' (24:63), since his commands are not his
own but those of Allah (SWT).

His Lord took an oath to withdraw faith from anyone who objects
to the Prophet's judgement when it is sought. 'By your Lord, they
will never [truly] believe until they make you [O Prophet], judge
concerning the disputes among themselves and find within themselves
no objection to what you have judged and submit willingly' (4:650).
Equally, He denied the faith of those who seek judgement from anyone
other than the Prophet.

It is evident from this that Prophet Muhammad (PBUH) is the
intention behind the creation and the high aim of the divine, where
He took the covenant of all His messengers from Adam to Jesus (peace
be upon them) to believe in Muhammad (PBUH) alongside the belief
in Allah (SWT) and support him.

---

[3]   The devil was asked to prostrate to Adam but refused out of arrogance,
       citing his superiority above him, since he was created from smokeless
       fire, while Adam (AS) was created from clay.

[4]   Adam.

And when Allah took the covenant of the Prophets (saying to them): 'Behold that which I have given you of the Scripture and wisdom and then there comes to you a Messenger confirming what is with you, you must believe in him and support him.' He [Allah then] said: 'Have you acknowledged and undertaken My covenant?' They replied, 'We have acknowledged it.' He said: 'Then bear witness, and I am with you among the witnesses.' (3:81)

And He preferred the Prophet (PBUH) above all the Messengers despite the oneness of the message: 'We make no distinction between any of His Messengers [as regards to their message]' (2:285). Thus, Allah (SWT) appointed him as the best of Prophets.

Oh Fatimah, our Prophet is the best of Prophets, and he is your father. And our martyr is the best of martyrs, and he is the uncle of your father.[5] From us is the one given wings, and able to fly in paradise wherever he wishes, and he is the son of the uncle of your father.[6] From us are the masters of the youth of paradise, the two grandchildren of this Ummah, Al-Hasan and Al-Hussein, and they are your sons. By Him Who sent me with Truth, their father is superior to them;[7] and from among us is the Mahdi.[8]

And He (SWT) made him a Prophet prior to completing the creation of Adam (AS), the patriarch of humanity. It is mentioned in a sound Hadith: 'I was appointed a Prophet, while Adam was between soul and body.'[9] He joined His name with the Prophet (PBUH) in the profession of faith and worship of Him, specifically in the most important aspects, the prayer and its call.[10] Moreover, Allah (SWT) made obedience to the Messenger obedience to Him (SWT),

---

[5] Hamza (RA), who was martyred in the Battle of Uhud.

[6] Ja'far bin Abu Talib, known as Ja'far at-Tayyar (the one able to fly).

[7] Ali (AS).

[8] Majma az-Zawaid.

[9] At-Tirmidhi.

[10] Adhaan.

allegiance to the Messenger allegiance to Him, and actions of the Messenger, His actions. And He will not welcome into His mercy the one whose heart is deprived of love for Muhammad (PBUH) since there is no faith without love for the Prophet and his family.

O Allah, we are unable to send prayers upon him as you wish for us to do. So you, O Allah, send prayers upon him and his family. He is your beloved, from whom you will accept intercession for those who deserve your wrath.

> When the disgraced is goaded to Hell
> Is there other than Ahmad who will avail and grant refuge?

O Allah, allow us to attain the outcome of his love, until we hear and see none but him. The beloved (PBUH)—due to his compassion—disclosed to us some of the attributes that Allah (SWT) gifted him with for us to recognise his noble status and keep us from diminishing it; repentance is forbidden for those that do! He (PBUH) is the one who set the best example of humility, the preeminent in dispensing with the worldly life to the extent of patching his own clothes, repairing his own sandals, and sleeping upon pillows of palm fibre. With all of this, he once said, indicating his elevated status and high rank above all messengers, 'Had Moses been amongst us, he would have to follow me,'[11] This was mentioned whilst Umar bin al-Khattab was reading a page of the book of the Jews.

The Prophet (PBUH) said:

> 'Adam and everyone related to him, will be under my flag
> [on the Day of Judgement], and this is not to boast';[12]

> 'My Lord has raised me, and perfected my upbringing';[13]

---

[11]   Musnad Ahmad.

[12]   Musnad Ahmad.

[13]   As-Shawkani, Fuad al-Majmuah.

'I am the city of knowledge, and Ali is its gate';[14]

'I am the master of humanity on the day of resurrection, and this is not to boast';[15]

'I am the gatherer, at my feet will be gathered all of humanity';[16] 'By the One in Whose Hand my soul resides, had one of you situated himself between the Black Stone and the Station of Ibrahim,[17] standing for worship, prayed, fasted and died upon this, yet had hatred for us: the family of Muhammad, will enter the fire';[18]

'I am unlike any one of you, it is my Lord Who always sustains me, and quenches my thirst'.[19]

Despite all of this, they say that he has no superiority over the other messengers, and they attribute to him the statement 'Let none of you say that I am better than Yunus Bin Matta.'[20] They submit infallibility to the narrator and wage war against those who reject it, attempting to reduce his lofty status despite Allah (SWT) saying, 'And be not like the companion of the whale [Prophet Yunus Bin Matta], when he called out while he was distressed' (68:48). This is despite the fact that Allah (SWT) himself confirms the superiority of some of the messengers above others. 'Those Messengers—we preferred some above others' (2:253). And above all them is the beloved Prophet Muhammad (PBUH). Insistence upon the authenticity of this false Hadith entails diminishing his status from being superior to Yunus (AS) and not out of love for him!

---

[14] Majma' az-Zawaid.

[15] Musnad Ahmad.

[16] Sahih al-Bukhari.

[17] Glass-and-metal enclosure with what is said to be an imprint of Abraham's foot.

[18] Majma' az-Zawaid.

[19] Sahih ibn Hibban.

[20] Musnad Ahmad.

They concocted a stance that the devil has influence upon the Prophet (PBUH) whilst negating it for one of his companions[21] whichever path he takes! It is alleged that the devil interjected upon his tongue whilst he was reading Chapter 53 in his prayer, negating his infallibility:[22] 'Those are the elevated cranes: truly their intercession is dearly hoped.'

Hence, they allege that he uttered satanic verses.[23] This is their interpretation of the verse, justifying their assertion: 'Never have We sent a Messenger or a Prophet before you but when He recited [the revelation] Satan interjected in his recitation' (22:52). They made up this stance despite this statement of Allah (SWT): 'Your companion (Muhammad) has not strayed, nor has he erred. Nor does he speak with any inclination. It is only revelation, revealed to him' (53:3–4). This is in the very same chapter in which they attributed the interjection of the devil upon his tongue! These attributions have led many non-Muslims to mock the most honourable of all creation based on these traditions claiming that he uttered satanic verses!

It is also alleged that the devil, on another occasion, provoked him whilst he was standing for prayer before Allah (SWT), interrupting him, coercing him to fight and suppress it: 'I seized it (the devil), and I felt the coldness of its tongue upon the back of my hands. Had it not been for the supplication of my brother Solomon, I would have shown it to you, bound to the pillar.'[24] All the while, the Prophet's (PBUH) statement regarding Umar bin al-Khattab is accepted with open arms: 'He never walks a path, except that the Devil takes a different path from his.'[25]

These two hadiths are in clear contradiction to authentic creed since they would indicate that the Prophet (PBUH), the teacher of

---

21   This companion being Umar bin al-Khattab.

22   Lubab An-Nuqul Li-Suyuti.

23   The title of the infamous book written by Salman Rushdie. It may surprise some readers to learn that the source of this title is found within Islamic literature!

24   Tarikh Baghdad.

25   Sahih al-Bukhari.

humanity, is lesser in status than the one who takes knowledge from him to begin with! Moreover, it would suggest that the relationship between his companion Umar and Allah (SWT) is stronger than that between the Messenger and Allah, who has chosen him to guide Umar from polytheism and the burying of his daughter alive[26] to faith in Allah (SWT) and His Messenger! How is it possible that the devil would flee from Umar but stand in the way of the Messenger of Allah (PBUH)? If the accuracy of these two hadiths is maintained, then on whom rests the support of Allah (SWT)—to the one from whom the devil flees or the one with whom the devil fights and whose prayers the devil stands in the way of?

It is further proposed that when Allah (SWT) sent the Prophet (PBUH), he had a disbelieving devil. But by the support of Allah (SWT), it converted to Islam and only commanded him to do good! In other words, he received commands for good works from a Muslim devil. How then can one separate between the sources of these commands? And what were their limits? Do they include sharia[27] since the sharia is a source of good just as the Qur'an is good?

It is mentioned in Sahih Muslim that Aisha said, 'The Prophet (PBUH) said to me: "Did your Devil come to you?" I said "Oh Messenger of Allah, do I have a devil?" He said: "Yes." I asked: "Does every human being also?" He said: "Yes." I then asked: "Do you have a devil also?" He replied: "Yes, but my Lord has supported me against it, and it has become Muslim."'[28]

Another Hadith states, '"None of you are free from an assigned Devil from the Jinn."[29] They asked: "What about you, Oh Messenger of Allah?"; he responded: "Me too, except that Allah has supported me

---

[26] A custom that was practised by some of the Arabs before the advent of the Prophet (PBHH) due to the shame brought upon the family by the birth of a daughter!

[27] The moral code and religious law of Islam.

[28] Sahih Muslim.

[29] Spiritual creatures (made from smokeless fire), who inhabit an unseen world in dimensions beyond the visible realm of humans.

against it, and it has become Muslim, and commands me with only good.'"[30]

In addition, it is mentioned that the devil flows within the Messenger, like the flowing of blood; it is reported in Musnad of Ahmad: "'Don't enter the chambers of women whose husbands are absent, since the devil flows in you through the blood vessels." We replied: "And in you too, Oh Messenger of Allah?" He said: "Yes, but my Lord has helped me against it, so it has become Muslim.'"[31]

Thus, the picture painted of the noble Messenger is one whose words—perhaps even the holy Qur'an—could be from the interjection of the devil upon his tongue. In this case, the Sunnah—if not the holy Qur'an—has the possibility, as claimed, to be from the orders of the 'good commanding devil'! Therefore, they believe in the Hadith of the inkpot and the shoulder bone[32] and consider the actions and statements of Umar as authentic when he said about the Prophet (PBUH) 'The Messenger has been overtaken by the pain'[33] and in his statement 'Indeed, he is hallucinating!' and rejected taking his words seriously. This cannot be, except by holding a view permitting his fallibility in delivering the message. Moreover, Umar made the statement 'The book of Allah is sufficient for us'!

They said that Umar was right and was advocating the truth for the sake of Allah and His Messenger! Thus according to this position, the verse of warning against disobeying the command of the Messenger for them is 'Let them beware, those who disobey the command of Umar even if it is against the Prophet'! Infallibility of the Messenger is

---

[30]   At-Tirmidhi.

[31]   Musnad Ahmad.

[32]   Al-Katf Wa-Dawah: this is a famous Hadith in Islam about an event when Umar prevented the Prophet's companions from obeying him to write his will of protection to the umma.

[33]   Sahih al-Bukhari.

a nonentity for them since the devil is able to interject upon his tongue and a Jew is able to befuddle his intellect with magic.[34]

Is the devil that interjected upon his tongue a Muslim devil or some other devil? The verses of the 'cranes' are undeniably ungodly. This would indicate that, indeed, there is another devil that did not accept Islam and had influence upon him, commanding the Messenger to evil! Or perhaps it was the same Muslim devil who happened to be a hypocrite, displaying Islam openly whilst concealing its disbelief? We seek the forgiveness of Allah (SWT); there is neither might nor strength except through Him!

---

[34] As mentioned in Hadiths that assert the Prophet (PBUH) being inflicted with magic to the point where he is unable to remember his actions.

3

The Accusation of Resorting to a Priest

It is mentioned in Sahih al-Bukhari:

> On the authority of Aishah—the mother of the believers—
> who said: 'The beginning of revelation to the Messenger
> of Allah (PBUH) was in the form of pious dreams during
> sleep. He used to not see a dream except that it came true
> as the break of dawn. Then seclusion was made beloved to
> him. He used to seclude himself in the cave of Hira and
> perform "tahannuth", meaning worshipping for many
> nights—before returning to his family. He used to take
> with him provisions for this and return to Khadija and
> then prepare his provisions for another seclusion until
> the truth came to him while he was in the cave of Hira.
> The angel came to him and said: "Read." The Prophet
> replied, "I am not a reader." The Prophet said, "The angel
> grabbed me and pressed me until it was unbearable. He
> then released me and said 'Read,' and I replied, 'I am not
> a reader.' Thereupon he grabbed me again and pressed me
> a second time until it was unbearable. He then released me
> and again asked me to read but again I replied, 'I am not
> a reader.' He then released me for the third time, and said:
> 'Read in the name of your Lord, who created. Created man
> from a clot [of blood]. Read! And your Lord is the Most

Generous.'" Then the Messenger of Allah (PBUH) returned with this [revelation] while his heart was beating severely. He went to Khadija bint Khuwailid (RA) and said, "Cover me! Cover me!" They covered him until his fear subsided. Thereafter, he told her everything that had happened and said, "I fear for myself." Khadija replied, "Never! By Allah, He will never disgrace you. You maintain family ties, you shoulder the weary, you provide for the deprived, you serve your guests generously and assist the misfortunate ones." Khadija then took him to her cousin Waraqa bin Nawfal bin Asad bin Abdul Uzza, who, during the pre-Islamic period became a Christian and was proficient in Hebrew. He would write from the Gospel in Hebrew as much as Allah willed. He was an old man and had become blind. Khadija said to Waraqa, "Oh my cousin, listen to the story of your nephew." Waraqa said, "O my nephew, what have you seen?" So the Messenger of Allah (PBUH) informed him of what he had seen. Waraqa said, "This is the Namus [i.e. Gabriel], whom Allah had sent to Moses. Oh how I wish I were young and could live up to the time when your people expel you." The Messenger of Allah (PBUH) replied, "Will they drive me out?" Waraqa replied in the affirmative and said, "No one came with something similar to what you have brought except that he was treated with enmity; and if I should remain alive until the day when you will be expelled, then I will support you wholeheartedly." But after a little while, Waraqa passed away and the Divine Inspiration ceased for a period of time.'[1]

The stones of Makkah would greet the Messenger of Allah (PBUH), professing his prophethood, before revelation began. The Messenger knew that he was a prophet even whilst Adam was being fashioned from clay! This truth is not far-fetched since Jesus (AS) was aware that he was a prophet whilst he was an infant in his mother's lap. 'They said, "How can we speak to a child in the cradle?" He [Jesus] said, "Indeed, I am the servant of Allah. He has given me the Scripture

---

[1]   Sahih Al-Bukhari.

and made me a Prophet'" (29:30). Thus, why would the Messenger (PBUH) be in need of resorting to a Christian priest to interpret for him what happened to him after the episode with Gabriel (AS)?

Moreover, they attribute to him the Hadith of excommunication of the one who resorts to a priest. 'Whomever approaches a priest or a fortune teller, and believes in what he says, has disbelieved in what is revealed to Muhammad (PBUH).'[2] Is what is to be understood from this Hadith that the Prophet (PBUH) would forbid an action and do it himself? That he forbade the visiting of a priest, yet it was the first thing he did after the revelation began? Thus, the portrait of the Messenger (PBUH) in their eyes is that of a psychologically ill individual searching for a remedy at the hands of a Christian priest! How can the one who accepts such a Hadith be able to defend the Prophet (PBUH)?

The Hadith proclaims, 'The Messenger of Allah (PBUH) returned with this [revelation] while his heart was beating severely. He went to Khadija bint Khuwailid (RA) and said, "Cover me! Cover me!" They covered him until his fear subsided. Thereafter, he told her everything that had happened and said, "I fear for myself."'

The Islamic resources have thus painted this picture of the Messenger (PBUH), who knew that he was a prophet whilst Adam (AS) was between his soul and body! Would he fear the vision of Gabriel (AS)? Did Gabriel (AS) present himself to him in the most horrid of forms? Indeed, if Gabriel (AS) would present himself to the Messenger (PBUH), he would do so in the most beautiful of human form, resembling, as said, that of Dihyah al-Kalbi.[3]

And if—for argument's sake—he did present to the Messenger (PBUH) in such a horrid form, would the Prophet's fearlessness abandon him? Is there one who is more fearless and braver than the Messenger of Allah (SWT) in opposition to an enemy? When the

---

2   Musnad Ahmad.

3   The envoy who delivered the Prophet's message to the Roman Emperor Heraclius.

companions would be overwhelmed by fear at night, they would find the Messenger (PBUH) coming back to them—from the direction of danger—on his mule, reassuringly saying, 'Don't be frightened.' Yet the sources of Islam render the Messenger (PBUH) as someone who seeks to cover himself with garment due to the depth of his fear; all the while, Allah (SWT) negates fear from his messengers, saying, 'Indeed, in My presence the Messengers do not fear' (27:10)!

Thus, there is nothing to glean from such a Hadith except to display the Messenger (PBUH) in a negative light of fear and weakness and to cast doubt on to him that he is the Messenger to all humanity and that he requires the guarantee of another for recognising Gabriel (AS), the Namus who came to Moses. On the other hand, Moses (AS) spoke directly to Allah (SWT);[4] He did not even send upon him the Namus, i.e. Gabriel (AS)!

---

[4] 'And Allah spoke directly to Moses' (4:164).

4

The Accusation of Attempting to Commit Suicide

It is reported in a Hadith *that Aisha said*:

> It wasn't long after Waraqa died and the Divine Revelation ceased. The Prophet became so sad—it has reached us—that he intended several times to throw himself from the peaks of high mountains and each time he reached the top in order to throw himself off, Gabriel would appear to him and say, 'O Muhammad! You truly are the Messenger of God,' and so his heart would become composed and he would calm down and return [home]. And whenever time between Revelations lengthened, he would do as before, but when reaching the mountain top, Gabriel would appear to him and say what he had said before.[1]

Can this state of affairs be attributed to the Messenger (PBUH), upon whom stones articulated their greetings even before revelation began? Likewise confirming his prophethood, he (PBUH) said, 'I was a Prophet while (the creation of) Adam was between soul and body.'[2]

---

[1] Sahih al-Bukhari.
[2] Mustadrak Ala Shahihayn.

Are they telling us that the Messenger (PBUH), after revelation, was afflicted by depression to the extent of having suicidal ideations when he is the soother of hearts, the radiance of the eyes, and the cure of the body? Is this how scholars of Islam see the person of the Prophet (PBUH)?

What is present in al-Bukhari is irrefutable in their eyes, as if infallibility is attributed to al-Bukhari and not the Messenger (PBUH)! Thus, the perception of the Messenger in the eyes of those scholars who attest to the infallibility of al-Bukhari and Muslim equates to that of an enemy. They paint a picture of the Messenger as a depressed individual who attempts to throw himself off the mountaintop, and claim that this is the Prophet of the Muslims. This is in defiance of the statement of Allah (SWT) regarding him as 'a healing for what is in the breasts' (10:57).

What is significant regarding the context of the above-mentioned Hadith is that the narrator is Aisha (RA) and the so-called incidence of attempted suicide occurred in Makkah. How old was Aisha (RA) when Waraqa passed away? If the case is true, then her age (according to the sources) is six or nine when she's in Medina. Then at what time did she hear this Hadith, or did the Messenger (PBUH) subsequently reveal to her that he attempted to commit suicide? We seek refuge in Allah (SWT) from such fabrications! Moreover, what is the significance of Waraqa in the Hadith? Are they suggesting that the Prophet (PBUH) depended upon what was related by Waraqa and that the revelation was a deceptive matter?

It's beyond me how these 'scholars of sharia' accept—to this day— everything they hear and then reiterate them to their students and upon the pulpits without flinching or batting an eyelid!

5

The Accusation of Being Bewitched

It is recorded in Sahih al-Bukhari:

> On the authority of Aisha (RA) who said: 'The Messenger
> of Allah was bewitched by a man from the tribe of Bani
> Zurayq—said to be Labid Bin Al-A'sam—until the
> Messenger (PBUH) used to imagine that he would carry
> out an action that he had not. One day on the morning or
> evening that he was with me, he supplicated to Allah for a
> long period then said; "O Aisha, do you know that Allah
> has informed me concerning the matter I have asked him
> about?" Two men came to me and one of them sat near my
> head, while the other at my feet. One of them said to the
> other, "What is the disease of this man?" The other replied,
> "He is affected by magic." The first one asked, "Who has
> done this upon him?" It was said, "Labid Bin Al-A'sam."
> The first one questioned again, "What did he use?" The
> other replied, "A comb and the hairs stuck to it and the skin
> of pollen of a male date palm." It was asked, "Where is it?"
> The other replied, "It is in the well of Dharwan." Thus,
> Allah's Messenger (PBUH) along with some companions
> went there and back, and he either said, "O Aisha, the
> colour of its water is like the infusion of Henna leaves", or
> (he said), "the tops of the date-palm trees near it are like

the heads of devils". I asked, "O Messenger of Allah, should you not show it (to the people)?" He said, "Since Allah has cured me, I dislike letting evil spread among the people." Then he ordered that the well be filled up with earth.'[1]

Only an unjust person affirms the bewitching of the Messenger (PBUH), as Allah (SWT) affirms, 'When the unjust say, "You follow not but a man bewitched [by magic]." See what portrayals they depict for you; so they have gone astray, and cannot find a way' (17:47–48). Allah (SWT) also says, 'And Allah will protect you from people' (5:67). If the Qur'an is used to thwart magic, then indeed the Messenger (PBUH) is the 'walking Qur'an'[2] since 'his character was the Qur'an'.[3] Had it been said that it was Aisha (to whom the Hadith is attributed) who was bewitched or Abu Bakr or Umar, then it would have been more appropriate since it is the Messenger (PBUH) who remedies the bewitched.

Notice the perception of the Messenger's character in the eyes of people who accept such narrations—a man who doesn't know what he has done or what he is doing! For how long did this situation last, and how can there be any reliance upon what was sent down to the Messenger during such a time, and how can it be discerned? Is all this attributed to the Messenger (PBUH), who was sent down by Allah (SWT) for the guidance of creation? Can a man from the tribe of Bani Zurayq play with the mind of the Messenger and influence his actions? Indeed, the prophet Moses (AS) thwarted the magic of those whom Allah (SWT) confirmed came with tremendous magic by means of his staff, without even reciting a verse of scripture upon them! The question arises, is the exalted Mohammedan essence less than that of the staff of Moses?

Undeniably, it is through the tongue of the Messenger that the statement of Allah issues forth, 'And the magician will not succeed no matter what he aim' (20:69). By what means then can a magician have

---

[1]   Sahih al-Bukhari.

[2]   As mentioned in the description of the messenger by his companions.

[3]   Musnad Ahmad.

influence upon the noblest Messenger of God? Is this how an 'excellent pattern of example'[4] is understood? Would Allah (SWT) command humanity to take from the Messenger (PBUH) whilst he is unaware of his actions? What then of this statement of Allah (SWT): 'And whatever the Messenger consigns unto you, take it, and from whatever he forbids you, abstain' (59:7).

---

[4]   See verse 33:21.

6

The Accusation of Doubting the Resurrection of the Dead

It is mentioned by the Prophet (PBUH) in a Hadith: 'Learn certainty.'[1] It is reported that Imam Ali (AS) said, 'Patience is the centre-poll of religion, and the best of faith is certainty.'[2] Thus, faith, if it reaches its peak, becomes certain and removes any doubts and suppositions. Faith increases and decreases until certainty settles this fluctuation. Certainty is attained by learning, and thus an informed teacher is essential. This spiritual development on the road to certainty includes practice since theoretical knowledge alone leads the person to faith but not to certainty. And the practice necessitates a spiritual guide who is well acquainted with the stations and obstacles along the path between faith and certainty. Moreover, faith pertains to the unseen and therefore is reflective knowledge having to do with abstract perceptions and not the realm of matter.

Allah (SWT) is the Knower of the unseen and the visible;[3] hence, the unseen is termed as such as far as creation is concerned. Since nothing is hidden from Allah (SWT), the unseen is inapplicable

---

[1] Tabaqat Ashafiiyyah.

[2] Yaqin.

[3] Ghayb Wa Shahadah.

27

to Him. Everything pertaining to Allah (SWT) is visible since He is the Creator of all that exists. Therefore, the unseen in relation to the creation is that which an individual yearns examination and understanding of in the search for certainty. If a person reaches the level of yearning to understand the unseen, the existence of the unseen becomes certainty for him, and so he yearns for its comprehension. This is termed *knowledge of certainty*,[4] and beyond this rests *truth of certainty*[5] and *essence of certainty*.[6] All these stations are possible for the human being unless he denies them. However, if one denies the unseen, he or she remains stagnant where they are in their faith and understanding. 'And the deniers thereupon, will lose everything' (40:78).

Knowledge—its depository is the realm of the unseen. Therefore, the denier of the unseen stands in opposition to exploration and contemplation, which is in fact peerless worship. Moreover, denial only inflates one's ignorance since it is not knowledge. It is reported in a tradition: 'An hour of contemplation is better than a year of worship.'[7] Allah (SWT), in the Qur'an, praises those who contemplate. 'Contemplating upon the creation of the heavens and the earth, [saying] 'Our Lord, You did not create all this purposeless; how exalted are You; protect us from the punishment of the Fire' (3:191). Imam Junaid (RA) was asked regarding the best of assemblies; he replied: 'The assemblies of contemplation in the domain of Tawhid.'[8]

If one reaches the station of certainty, doubt will cease to exist for him. It is reported that Ali (AS), the commander of the believers, mentioned, 'Had veils (of the unseen) been revealed to me, I would not increase in certainty.' This intimates to the utmost level of certainty that neither increases or decreases and is not swayed by temporal events as is the case with the majority of people!

---

4   Ilm Ul Yaqin.
5   Haq Ul Yaqin.
6   Ayn Ul Yaqin.
7   Al-Lulu al-Marsu'.
8   Monotheism.

The messengers are the paragons of their communities that Allah (SWT) chose for them. Had there been one who is superior amongst their community, it would be more appropriate for that person to be chosen by Allah (SWT). Thus, it is inconceivable that He (SWT) would select for himself a messenger when another was superior in knowledge, form, and character. Yet this position is maintained by those who give preference—in certain circumstances—to a companion above the greatest of all Prophets during differences of opinions, claiming that Allah (SWT) supported this companion whilst reproaching His Prophet (PBUH)! This is akin to inverting the meaning of the verse Allah (SWT) said to His Messenger: 'Let those who contravene the order of that companion be warned; or Whatever that companion consigns unto you, take it!'

The messengers are indeed the perfect words of Allah (SWT); through them He delivers His servants from the recesses of darkness to the light, and from amongst them is Jesus (AS). 'The Messenger of Allah and His word which He bestowed on Mary, and a spirit from Him' (4:171). They guide the creation by the hand to faith and certainty from the cesspit of doubt and bitter inconstancy. Thus, it is beyond the bounds of possibility to ascribe doubt regarding their message to any of the chosen messengers after being chosen by Allah (SWT) to guide His servants to Him.

Whosoever claims anything on the contrary to this places himself as having knowledge and authority above the prophets and messengers, decreeing this position upon them with his own limited understanding! Hence, he becomes arrogant and feels superior due to knowledge that is impossible to be given to him. Why would Allah veil this knowledge from His chosen messengers, those that He created for himself, made beloved, and sent prayers upon the greatest of them?

The greatest of the messengers of Allah (SWT) is claimed to have said: 'We are more deserving of doubt than Abraham (AS).'[9] And then the following verse of Allah (SWT) is provided as explanation: 'And when Abraham said, "My Lord, show me how You give life to

---

[9]   Sahih al-Bukhari.

the dead." Allah said, "Do you not believe?" He said, "Yes, but for the contentment of my heart"' (2:260). It is thought by many that Abraham (AS) doubted the ability of Allah (SWT) in resurrecting the dead! Whoever holds this to be true has in fact left the fold of Islam because he anathematises from Islam not only a prophet but the father of prophets.[10]

Attempts are made to mitigate this understanding by claiming that Abraham (AS) had doubt that Allah (SWT) would answer his question! This is absurd since Allah (SWT) says, 'And when My servants ask you (Oh Muhammad) about Me, then I am near; responding to the supplication of the supplicator when he calls. So let them respond to Me, and believe in Me, so that they may be guided' (2:186). Moreover, when the devil asked Allah (SWT), He responded, 'He [the devil] said, "My Lord, reprieve me until the Day they are resurrected." He [Allah] said, "You are of those who are reprieved, until the Day of the known time"' (15:36–38). So how can the father of the prophets have doubt regarding whether Allah (SWT) would respond to him whilst having the epithet the *friend of Allah* (SWT)?

In fact, Abraham (AS) did not question the competence of the divine ability. God forbid. Rather, his question testifies to the depth of his faith since he requested to know *how* the dead are brought back to life. The request to know the how indicates his certainty of its occurrence, albeit without the knowledge of the means. The knowledge of how is through a practical example, and therefore his question is a request for tutelage regarding the resurrection of the dead. This matter is possible for all those who have reached the status of *khullah*,[11] or intimacy with Allah (SWT), the status of Abraham (AS). Whoever enters upon this status is safe from everything[12] and therefore would never do an action and worry about its imperfection.

---

10 Prophet Abraham is referred to as the patriarch of the prophets in the Islamic tradition.

11 Khullah is the status of being *khalil*, 'intimate friend'.

12 Wherein are plain messages of guidance: 'The station of Abraham; and whosoever enters it is safe' (3:97).

In this state, one is able to resurrect the dead, as Jesus (AS) used to do. Despite Abraham (AS) having reached this position, 'And Allah took Abraham as an intimate friend (4:125), he had not attempted to raise the dead. Thus, he requested permission from Allah (SWT): 'My Lord, show me how You give life to the dead' (2:260). The response of Allah (SWT) was the question 'Do you not believe?' This was not about doubt in the divine ability or faith in the divine; in fact, the one who has reached the level of intimate friend deserves and is able to resurrect the dead. This was known to Abraham (AS) and to whomever Allah (SWT) favoured with His mercy. Hence, Allah's (SWT) question of 'Do you not believe?' was in fact testimony from Allah (SWT) that he (Abraham) had the right to raise the dead, so away with these doubts, i.e. 'Do you not believe that you are from this honoured level and My "intimate friend"?' Abraham replied, "Yes." In other words, 'I have faith in this, Oh Lord, but for the contentment of my heart' with a testimony from you. 'He (SWT) said: Take four birds and usher them towards yourself. Then [after slaughtering] put on each mountain a portion of them; then call upon them—they will come to you in haste. And know that Allah is Exalted and Wise' (2:260). And thus, Abraham set out in earnest to raise the dead by himself, which was the purpose of his initial question of 'How?'—a matter far from doubt by Abraham (AS), the intimate friend of Allah (SWT). None can hold such a position except one who shoulders the worst of knowledge. How dare they!

Yet with this type of knowledge, they fabricated a sheer lie and said that the greatest of messengers said, 'We are more deserving of doubt than Abraham (AS).' Grave are the words that come out of their mouths! If the messengers are in doubt regarding faith and certainty, then who would teach humankind and acquaint them with Allah (SWT)? With all this, they try to affirm doubt on Abraham (AS) and the best of messengers (PBUH).

Ironically, if doubtful faith is attributed to one who holds such a position, the response would be one of total denial or even violence. Nor is this doubt attributable to the four imams,[13] who are referred to

---

13   Al-Madhahib al-Arba'ah.

as sources of the religion. Yet the attribution of doubt to the Messenger is admissible! O Allah (SWT), we exonerate ourselves from attributing doubt to your messengers in their faith and shortcomings in their certainty.

7

The Accusation of Smearing Abraham, a Prophet of Allah, with Lying

It is attributed by al-Bukhari that Abraham, whom Allah (SWT) described as being of beautiful character, 'lied not, except three lies.'[1]

From the outset, the requisite qualities of messengers are as follows: honesty, trustworthiness, conveyance (of their message), and supreme intelligence. What is inconceivable for them are lies, betrayal, secrecy (of the truth), and stupidity; hence, it is beyond the majesty of Allah (SWT) to send a messenger that lies! Indeed, the noblest Messenger (PBUH) was once asked, '"Can a believer be a coward?" He responded saying: 'Yes.' It was asked: 'Can a believer be a miser?' He replied: 'Yes.' It was then asked: 'Can a believer be a liar?' He said: 'No"'[2]

Thus, there remains no character nor positive quality for one who lies! Then how can the concocter of such a Hadith intend it to be an evidence for the Messenger of Allah (PBUH), testifying to the lies of one of the *ulul adham*,[3] Abraham (AS)? The tone of the Hadith

---

[1] Sahih Al-Bukhari.

[2] Alistidhkar ibn Abdul Barr.

[3] One of the five most prominent prophets. These prophets are favoured by Allah and are described in the Qur'an to be endowed with

33

suggests that three lies are an easy affair that can be disregarded: 'except three lies' only! All the while, Allah (SWT) describes Abraham (AS) in His holy scripture: 'And mention in the book, Abraham. Indeed, he was a truthful Prophet' (19:41).

The Hadith is intended to support the following:

1. The prophets lie, and three lies of a prophet are unobjectionable.

2. The one who testifies to these lies is none other than the Messenger, Muhammad (PBUH), and he attributes them to one of the *ulul adham*, Abraham (AS).

3. According to the Hadith of al-Bukhari, Abraham (AS) lies; therefore, he has no faith, as confirmed by the Messenger (PBUH): 'The ones who invent falsehood are those who do not believe' (16:105).

4. The Messenger (PBUH), as mentioned in Sahih al-Bukhari, contradicts the Qur'an. And Allah (SWT) says regarding Abraham (AS), 'And mention in the book, Abraham. Indeed, he was a truthful Prophet' (19:41), whereas Muhammad (PBUH) attributes to Abraham three lies!

If we add 'We are more worthy of doubt than Abraham (AS)'[4] to this Hadith, then the following meaning will be apparent: 'We are more worthy of lying than Abraham (AS)'! If indeed the messengers lie, then what is required of those to whom they were sent? Perhaps such hadiths are the reason for the diffusion of lies in the umma, whereas one will find in other communities—from the people of the book—if one were to attribute lies to them, there would be no offence greater than that for rebuke.

---

determination and perseverance. These prophets are Noah, Abraham, Moses, Jesus, and Muhammad. (Peace be upon them all.)

4   Sahih al-Bukhari.

8

The Accusation of Love for the Wife of Zaid (RA)

Allah (SWT) said:

> And when you said to the one on whom Allah bestowed upon favour and you bestowed favour upon, 'Hold on to your wife and be conscious of Allah,' and you concealed within yourself that which Allah will disclose. And you feared [for] the people, while Allah is more deserving of fear. So when Zaid had come to the end of his union with her, We married you to her so that there may not be upon the believers any discomfort concerning the wives of their adopted sons when they divorce them. And indeed, the command of Allah is always carried out. (33:37)

Some of the mufassirun, due to the false claim of knowledge, have fallen short of attaining the goal—for lack of love—of seeing the splendour of the one who has encompassed all knowledge. Hence, they believed that they had comprehended the speech of Allah (SWT), and they embarked on explanations based upon sick ideas, offering them up for the Muslims in their impure and harmful Qur'anic interpretations.[1] This is due to their failure to recognise the true status of the beloved and the limited perspectives of their tainted souls. Consequently, they have spoken about him as an ordinary person and have missed the aim of the divine in His revelation.

It is alleged, regarding the noblest of creation, that he desired for himself the wife of Zaid (RA) but hid this desire, fearing that it would become manifest to the people, and hence said to Zaid, 'Hold on to your wife' (33:37). This coincided with the inner desires of some due to the inclination and tendency of their hearts towards immorality. Indeed, it is mentioned in the tafsir of al-Qurtubi:[2]

> There is a difference of opinion regarding this verse.[3] Qatadah, Ibn Zaid, and the majority of Mufassirun, among them al-Tabari and others, held that the Prophet (PBUH) felt desire for Zaynab Bint Jahsh, while she was married to Zaid, and was eager for Zaid to divorce her so that he could marry her. Thereafter, when Zaid informed him of his desire to separate from her, complaining of her rudeness, her neglect of his requirements, her verbal abuse towards him, and inflating her nobility; the Prophet (PBUH) said to him: 'be conscious of Allah' i.e. regarding your statements about her, and 'Hold on to your wife', while concealing his eagerness for Zaid to divorce her. This is what he (the Prophet) concealed in his heart, but it is imperative on him to command only to goodness. It is also mentioned that, he feared the condemnation of the believers had he asked Zaid to divorce Zaynab, that they would say: 'He commands a man to divorce his wife then marries her straight after.'[4]

Nothing more heinous has been attributed to the Messenger of Allah (PBUH)—by arrogating to oneself to know what the Prophet (PBUH)

---

[1]   *Tafasir*: plural of Qur'anic interpretations.

[2]   Al-Qurtubi.

[3]   See verse 33:37.

[4]   Al-Qurtubi.

is concealing and then depicting it as: 'The Prophet (PBUH) felt desire for Zaynab Bint Jahsh, while she was married to Zaid, and was eager for Zaid to divorce her so that he could marry her.' This statement is then reiterated without shame: 'While concealing his eagerness for Zaid to divorce her. This is what he (the Prophet) concealed in his heart.' Is there a claim of knowing the unseen and what is concealed in the hearts greater than this? Is there an accusation of immorality and bad conduct more than this? Moreover, to attribute all this to the Messenger of Allah!

Nowhere does Allah (SWT) mention that the Prophet (PBUH) felt desire for a married woman or that he was eager for her divorce so that he could marry her. From where did this falsehood originate? How did this claim of divinity and 'pharaohnism'[5] by these mufassirun happen, that they know what lay in the heart of the Messenger of Allah (PBUH), and how was this accepted by Muslims? This allegation of knowing what lay in the Messenger's heart is an insult to their own selves by what they attribute to him (PBUH)!

All that Allah (SWT) disclosed was his marriage to Zaynab; therefore, what the Prophet (PBUH) concealed from Zaid was his knowledge that she is one of the wives that Allah (SWT) has decreed for him. This is what Allah (SWT) disclosed: 'So when Zaid had come to the end of his union with her, We married you to her' (33:37). Yet the mufassirun claim a knowledge of the unseen—the content of the Prophet's heart—which none knows except Allah (SWT) and His Messenger (PBUH). Moreover, with this claim, they accuse the Messenger (PBUH) of having immoral thoughts and disclose what he concealed; hence, they violated etiquette with Allah (SWT) and His Messenger (PBUH)! There is no greater claim to divinity and pharaohnism than this since none but Allah (SWT) knows what rests in His Messenger's heart (PBUH). Allah (SWT) says, 'Your Lord is most knowing of what is within yourselves' (17:25). Attributing this trait to any God-conscious person is obscene, so how can one be tempted to attribute it to the noblest of creation?

---

5   Since the claim of the pharaoh was that he was the greatest Lord.

In reality, Allah the Exalted has made apparent in this verse[6] the greatness of the status of the Messenger (PBUH) and his rank by specifying his favour alongside the favour of Allah (SWT). 'And when you said to the one on whom Allah bestowed upon favour and you bestowed favour upon' (33:37). This comes as no surprise, as Allah (SWT) has allowed for him likewise blessings that enrich just as Allah (SWT) has blessings that enrich! Allah (SWT) says, 'And they were not resentful except that Allah and His Messenger had enriched them [the Muslims] of His bounty' (9:74). He (SWT) also says, 'If only they had been satisfied with what Allah and His Messenger gave them, and said, "Allah is sufficient for us; Allah will give us of His bounty, and His Messenger also; indeed, we desire Allah"' (9:59). Moreover, Allah (SWT) has decreed that obedience to the Messenger is obedience to Him, and allegiance to the Messenger is allegiance to Him. 'Whoever obeys the Messenger has indeed obeyed Allah' (4:80). 'Behold, those who pledge their allegiance to you, have indeed pledged their allegiance to Allah, the hand of Allah is above their hands' (48:10).

The bearer of this most radiant station is praised by Allah (SWT). 'And indeed, you are of the most exalted integrity of morals' (68:4). So by what means can he be desirous of a woman who is already married and conceal this, fearing that it would become manifest to the people? A thing that one fears could become manifest to the people— it must be a sin![7] What was this offence that the Messenger (PBUH) concealed—as alleged—which was then disclosed by Allah (SWT)? Did He (SWT) inform us that Muhammad (PBUH) was in love with Zaynab whilst she was married to Zaid, concealing in this statement of his: 'Hold on to your wife and be conscious of Allah'? Then Allah (SWT) would humiliate His Prophet by disclosing to the people what he concealed!

---

6   33:37.
7   Referring to the Hadith: 'Righteousness is in good character, and wrongdoing is that which wavers in your heart, and which you dislike people finding out about.' Sahih Muslim.

By what means did the mufassirun satisfy themselves to utter these words? Anyone who seeks soundness of his religion would rise above this type of conduct, then how about the conduct of the standard reference of morality—outwardly and inwardly—who established the religion in the first place? 'Verily, in the Messenger of Allah you have the best example [to follow], for the one who looks forward [with hope and awe] to Allah and the Last Day and remembers Allah often' (33:21). Indeed, Allah (SWT) praised him for His supreme character; master of all of humanity, the possessor of the banner of praise, whom the prophets, Adam, and all those below him will be under!

Allah (SWT) says, 'And you feared (for) the people, while Allah is more deserving of fear.' What is this fear? Imam Ali (AS) said, 'We, whenever the heat of battle intensified, sought protection behind the Messenger of Allah (PBUH).' So what was this fear? Is it, as claimed, the fear of the people finding out about his concealed desire for Zaynab whilst she was married to Zaid? Is this how the verses of the Qur'an are interpreted in reference to the possessor of the greatest integrity of morals? What did Allah (SWT) manifest other than his marriage to her?

This verse was revealed in praise of the Messenger of Allah (PBUH), as mentioned earlier, by appointing for him favour alongside the favour of Allah (SWT). 'And when you said to the one on whom Allah bestowed upon favour and you bestowed favour upon.' Moreover, the Messenger (PBUH)—due to his high integrity of morals—ordered Zaid to hold on to his wife when he wanted to divorce her despite the fact that he knew she was from amongst the wives that Allah (SWT) had decreed for him. Thus, he (PBUH) concealed this knowledge from Zaid: 'And you concealed within yourself that which Allah will disclose' (i.e. the knowledge that Zaynab is amongst the wives decreed for him).

And this is what Allah (SWT) disclosed: 'So when Zaid had come to the end of his union with her, We married you to her' (33:37). It was not because of feelings of love for her, as interpreted by certain blameworthy individuals who have surrounded themselves with the pleasures of the world and its inclinations. They have been unable to fathom the profound Muhammadan purpose and character that was manifested over the exposure of his knowledge to Zaid, fearing that it would distress him had he informed him of this knowledge since Zaynab was still married to him. This is what is meant from the statement of Allah (SWT): 'And you fear (for) the people' (i.e. you fear that people may hear from you what might hurt them even though it is knowledge and truth)! Neither the diseased heart nor the weak mind were able to comprehend this; they failed to ascend to the level of recognition of the superiority of this character, and as a result, they descended into interpreting it in the context of love for women without any evidence, and then they have fabricated the claim of knowing what lies in the heart of the Prophet (PBUH) and accuse him of harbouring indecency!

Allah (SWT) says, 'While Allah is more deserving of your fear . . .', i.e. by manifesting the knowledge that Allah (SWT) disclosed to the Messenger (PBUH), 'I was sent as the teacher,'[8] so that Zaid and others know that Zaynab is amongst the wives decreed for him despite the fact that she was married to Zaid. Allah (SWT) says, 'Thereafter [unordained] women will not be lawful for you, nor for you to exchange them for other wives, even though their beauty might please you' (33:52). Yet your great integrity of morals, O Muhammad (PBUH), manifested over your knowledge, O city of knowledge. Allah (SWT) says, '[This is the] Manifestation of Allah. And who is better than Allah in manifesting [His religion]. And we worship only Him' (2:138).

Morality is the purpose of the Muhammadan message, and thus in the prophetic conduct, there exists only the apex of morality in all its facets. Whosoever sees other than this, may Allah (SWT) guide them! The conduct of the Prophet (PBUH) with Zaid (RA) was indeed the apex of morality, regarding which many have been unable to grasp! Knowledge is from the attributes of the divine, whilst morality is from the attributes of man. The Prophet (PBUH) attired his knowledge with morality and covered his splendour with beauty. 'Oh you who covered [his knowledge with morality]' (74:1). Absolute truth is

---

8   Ibn Majah.

majesty unendurable. 'If He removes it [the veil], the Light of His Face will burn every created thing that His sight reaches.'[9] But you, O Messenger of Allah (PBUH), are the bridge between divine truth and creation, between beauty and majesty, and you did not manifest of your essence for creation except beauty! Therefore, they all loved you, the divine and the creation; hence, you became the foundation of love.

Of gentleness, warmth, and mercy, you are the shining example; for covering humanity, presently and in the hereafter with your intercession, you are the garment. Due to your blessings upon them, you transformed their misery of sinning and repudiated the roots of their depression and despair since 'the Prophet has a greater claim over the believers than they have over themselves' (33:6). This is due to your eagerness for their refinement and purification. 'A Messenger has come to you from amongst yourselves. Grievous to him is your suffering; concerned over you and to the believers he is kind and merciful' (9:128). May the prayers and blessings of Allah (SWT) be upon you and your family and those who pray upon you.

In the verse 'Even though their beauty might please you' (33:52) is evidence for the supererogatory nature of the niqab,[10] as is also indicated in the verse 'Tell the believing men to lower their gaze' (24:30). Had the face been concealed with the niqab, then the verse would not have made this point. This attests to the fact that it is not compulsory upon the woman to conceal her face, in which case there would be no need to lower the gaze. Had it been the case, there would be more reason to conceal the face during worship and, in particular, during circumambulation during hajj and umrah.

---

9   Sahih Muslim.
10   *Niqab*: a cloth which veils the face of a woman.

9

The Accusations regarding
the Captives of Badr[1]

Allah (SWT) said, 'When you meet the unbelievers [in the battlefield], smite their necks until you have vanquished them, then bind them [as captives] firmly; thereafter set them free, either by an act of grace, or against ransom, but not before the end of the state of war' (47:4).

What is meant by 'the meeting' in the phrase 'When you meet the unbelievers' is war, and this only refers to those who are transgressors. The disbelievers[2] and polytheists, who are bent on denying the truth, are transgressors by nature against freedom of thought and religion. They insist upon forbidding people to choose or leave a belief. Moreover, they assault intellectuals and reformists. They ridiculed and mocked them and at times even killed them, just as had occurred to the prophets of Allah (SWT) throughout the passage of time. Thus, the divine command came to clarify the manner of war to be waged against them: 'Smite their necks until you have vanquished them, then bind them [as captives] firmly' (47:4). Vanquishing in war is, in fact,

---

[1] Badr: the first battle waged against the Messenger (PBUH) and his companions.

[2] *Disbelievers* here refer specifically to the leaders of Makkah at the time.

driving the enemy to a state of exhaustion so that some of its troops may give themselves up as captives due to the fear of death or that the victorious party who dominate the battlefield may take them as prisoners of war (POWs).

What is demanded of Muslims is to provide asylum to the captives and to not continue killing them and 'striking the necks' since the purpose behind war in Islam is not to eradicate the enemy but rather to defeat them. If victory becomes evident and the enemy is vanquished 'until you have vanquished them', then Muslims should take the defeated troops as captives. That is the statement of Allah (SWT), 'Then take them in captivity', which is taking POWs. Hence, Allah (SWT) prescribed the taking of captives in wars to preclude the eradication of the defeated enemies, albeit after vanquishing them since the captive is not put to death. And whoever is taken as a captive, it is imperative to behave towards him with beautiful conduct and to not kill him since the place of killing is in the arena of the battlefield.

Indeed, Allah (SWT) clarified the mode of conduct regarding captives after the battle, stating, 'Thereafter set them free, either by an act of grace, or against ransom.' Thus, there is no place in Islam for killing POWs; rather, dealing with them with courtesy and beautiful character is essential. Allah (SWT) did not commend those who killed the captives, nor did He prescribe it. On the contrary, He praised those who deal with POWs with beautiful character and described them as beloveds of Allah (SWT) due to this good conduct. 'Those who, for the love of Him, feed the needy, the orphan, and the captive' (76:8).

Allah (SWT) commanded His noble Messenger to address the captives of Badr and call them towards beautifying the conscience, resulting in beautiful human interaction, so they could be forgiven since religion is 'beautifying' human interaction.[3] Consequently, whoever beautifies his conscience, his morals, and his interactions likewise will become beautiful, and he becomes eligible for Allah's (SWT) grace, because it was moral character that the Prophet (PBUH) was sent to perfect. It is the aim of his message.

---

[3]   As mentioned in the Hadith, 'religion is [beautifying] human interaction'.

The aim of the message has been ignored or forgotten by many of those who speak for Islam. Talking about morality and beautiful interactions is less favoured amongst many of them since they ignore, disregard, or misunderstand why Muhammad (PBUH) was sent. Therefore, they incline towards praising one whose character is harsh, has rough interactions, and addresses people with the stick!

Allah (SWT) did not command the Prophet (PBUH) to be ill-mannered with the captives that were brought to him, not even to use harsh words, let alone to kill them. He (SWT) commanded the Prophet (PBUH) to address the captives, not to kill them! How then can it be said that He blamed him for not killing them? Allah (SWT) says, 'O Prophet! Say to the captives in your hands: "If Allah finds any goodness in your hearts He will give you that which is better than what has been taken away from you, and He will forgive you. Allah is Ever Forgiving, Most Merciful"' (8:70). This is the method of inviting them towards reformation that the Prophet of mercy came with.

Allah (SWT) did not order him to kill the captives who were in the hands of his companions if they did not testify that 'there is no God but Allah'! Similarly, he did not command the polytheists of Mecca, after the conquest of their city and having achieved victory over them, to testify that 'there is no God but Allah.' Rather, he left them free. 'Whoever wishes to believe, believe; and whoever wishes to disbelieve, disbelieve' (18:29). And from amongst them was Abu Sofian[4] and Muawiyah,[5] his son.

How honourable a message and how honourable a Prophet! Thus, he is the gift of mercy for all humanity; prayers and blessings of Allah (SWT) be upon him and his family. He's the establisher of human rights for both the living and the dead, irrespective of religion, race, or gender. Indeed, he stood in respect as a funeral once passed by; it was said to him the funeral was for a Jew. The Prophet (PBUH)

---

[4]   Sakhr ibn Harb ibn Umayyah—popularly known as Abu Sofian, Muawiya's father—who led the Quraysh army against the Prophet in the battles of Uhud and Khandaq.

[5]   Muawiyah: Muawiyah ibn Abi Sufyan was the first Umayyad caliph.

replied, 'Is he not a human being?'[6] It was once said to him, 'Oh Messenger of Allah (SWT), invoke curse upon the polytheists.' And he replied, 'I have not been sent to invoke curses, rather, I have been sent as mercy.'[7]

Therefore, if the mission of the Messenger (PBUH) has no room for cursing the polytheists, how can it accommodate such severity and harshness that would go as far as killing captives, the most in need of the mercy that Muhammad (PBUH), the Messenger of Allah (SWT), manifested?

The killing and taking of captives is not practised except by warriors in the battlefield, who may not adhere to the orders given by the highest leadership, just as the companions did in the Battle of Uhud.[8] The Prophet (PBUH) had instructed the archers not to leave their positions even if they witnessed him and those with him being snatched by raptors.

It is mentioned in Bukhari that the Prophet (PBUH) appointed Abdullah ibn Jubayr to be the leader of fifty archers on the day of the Battle of Uhud and commanded them to remain in their positions, saying, 'Even if you see us being snatched by raptors, do not abandon your posts, until you are discharged. And if you see us defeating the enemy and have vanquished them, do not abandon your posts, until you are discharged!' However, did the companions commit themselves to the command of the Prophet (PBUH)?

On the contrary, they did not obligate themselves to the instructions of the Prophet (PBUH) but openly disobeyed, paying no attention to his orders. Allah (SWT) affirmed this in His book when He said, 'And you have disobeyed [the Prophet] after He showed you what you intensely desire [i.e. victory]' (3:152). And this was despite the

---

6   Sahih al-Bukhari: the primary Hadith book of Sunni Muslims.

7   Sahih Muslim: the primary Hadith book of Sunni Muslims, which is second only to Bukhari, although there is a minor difference of opinion.

8   Uhud: the second battle waged against the Messenger (PBUH) and his companions.

Prophet (PBUH) emphasising with 'even if you see us being snatched by raptors'! In fact, this was the direct cause of their defeat in the Battle of Uhud.

Previously, in the Battle of Badr, the Prophet (PBUH) specified the positions in the battlefield where some of the polytheists that he named would be killed, and he commanded them to spare none save al-Abbas[9] (RA). It is related by Ibn Abbas that the Messenger (PBUH) said on the day of Badr, 'Whoever amongst you meets Al-Abbas should not fight him, indeed he came out under coercion.'[10] Yet what was done by the fighters in the battlefield? They hastened to capture the disbelievers when the glimmer of victory and defeat of the polytheists appeared since, in taking captives, there is material gain for the captor from booty and military equipment. Thus, they preferred taking captives before vanquishing them! Did they understand from the specification by the Prophet (PBUH) of the positions where the polytheists would be killed to mean to take them as captives?[11] The answer is clear.

Indeed, the indication from the Prophet (PBUH) was to vanquish the enemy in the battlefield and not to bring him captives. Similarly, the exemption of al-Abbas from being killed indicated vanquishing the enemy since the Prophet (PBUH) did not exempt any other except him. Yet the companions who were fighting preferred taking captives before vanquishing the enemy. They did not adhere to the Prophet's instructions nor to the divine command, which was to 'smite' the necks of the enemies until 'vanquishing'[12] is achieved and to take no captives before this.

Consequently, they were censured by Allah (SWT): 'You [in plural] merely seek the gains of this world' (8:67). The *gains of this world* in

---

[9]   Al-Abbas ibn Abd al-Muttalib was a paternal uncle of the Prophet (PBUH).

[10] Mustadrak.

[11] As indicated by the Hadith, the Prophet (PBUH) specified the exact place where each of the leaders of the disbelievers will fall in battle.

[12] Victory.

the verse is the material benefit that the captor may gain from what the captive brings of booty and wealth—the spoils of war. Yet they did not heed what was conveyed by the leader and teacher (PBUH), just as they did not heed what he explicitly said to them during the Battle of Uhud when he commanded them in the clearest terms not to abandon their positions. In both cases, they contravened and disobeyed him and did not commit themselves to his instructions despite his indisputable statement: 'Even if you see us being snatched by raptors! Thus, was the noble verse revealed, which censured them and attested to their disobedience: 'And you disobeyed [the Prophet] after He showed you what you intensely desire, for some of you sought this world and some of you sought the Next' (3:152).

With regard to the Battle of Badr, the address was directed to those who hastened towards getting hold of captives before achieving victory; it was said to them, 'You [in plural] merely seek the gains of this world whereas Allah desires [for you the good of] the Hereafter' (8:67). This was not directed to the Prophet (PBUH). Had it been so, the address would have been singular[13] and not plural.[14] Therefore, the censuring was aimed at those who disobeyed what the Prophet (PBUH) conveyed to them. It is inconceivable that the censuring in the verse, as held by many, is aimed at the Prophet (PBUH). This is because, in this situation, his knowledge of the obligation of killing the captives should have been before the event of taking them due to this statement of Allah (SWT): 'It is not for a Prophet to take captives until he has sufficiently suppressed the enemies in the land' (8:67).

This knowledge, by necessity, should be acquired via revelation prior to the event. He (PBUH)—as indicated in the Hadith—knew from Allah (SWT) before the battle that all prophets (peace and blessing be upon them) should kill captives and not accept ransoms; however, despite this, he acted in contrary to it. Hence, the censure will be for conduct that was contrary to the knowledge revealed to him prior to the event, that all prophets should kill the captives! This is what is understood from their interpretation of the verse! And had the

---

13   *Tureed* is singular.
14   *Tureeduna* is plural.

prophets formerly killed captives of war (and this was known to the Prophet), there would have been no need for consulting Abu Bakr,[15] Umar,[16] and Ali[17] regarding the captives, as mentioned in the Hadith, since there would be no need for their opinion in that case.

It is inconceivable for a Muslim to say that the infallible Prophet (PBUH) did not comply with what was revealed to him and that he behaved in the opposite way, contravening his Lord, the one who chose him from amongst his creation for his nobility and knowledge to establish the principles of law for all of humanity, and then contravening the traditions of the prophets that preceded him. It is mentioned in the Qur'an: 'Tell them [oh Prophet] . . . I only act upon what is revealed to me' (46:9). The reality is that the Prophet (PBUH) never commanded the soldiers to take the polytheists as captives. Then how can he be censured for taking captives when he did not command the combatants to take captives in the first place?

There's a big difference between taking captive a warrior who wants to kill you and killing a helpless captive whom you had no hand in capturing. The censuring in the verse is related to the capturing of the warriors and not the killing of the captives; these two matters are completely different since the captive hopes for mercy, whilst the fighter desires killing.

Then what happened, after the battle had unsatisfactorily ended the way it did, with regard to the combatants contravening the instructions of the Prophet (PBUH) and hastening to capture the enemy before vanquishing them and then going to the Prophet (PBUH) with seventy captives? The Hadith indicates that Umar was extremely eager to kill the captives; then why did he not kill them

---

[15] Abu Bakr bin Abi Quhafa, the first caliph and a member of the clan of Taym.

[16] Umar bin al-Khattab al-Adawi al-Qurashi, an early Meccan companion of the Prophet Muhammad and is the second caliph.

[17] Ali ibn Talib is the cousin and son-in-law of the Prophet (PBUH), is the father of the Prophet's grandsons Hasan (AS) and Husayn (AS), and is the fourth caliph.

in the battlefield prior to their arrival before the Messenger of Allah (PBUH)? And why did he not at the very least kill his relative whom he had sought permission from the Prophet (PBUH) to kill since the battlefield is the place of killing?

In fact, the captives were taken to Medina to be dealt with, as was mandatory, and not to be killed since only the battlefield is the arena of war and killing. What is mandatory in respect of dealing with captives is what Allah (SWT) commanded: 'Thereafter set them free, either by an act of grace, or against ransom' (48:4). This is the Mohammedan character since his character (PBUH) was the Qur'an.[18] He is sent as mercy to all creation, not only for the Muslims. Thus, all the actions of the Prophet (PBUH) are absolute truth since his essence is the truth and nothing emanates from the truth except truth.

Allah (SWT) mentions, 'How would Allah bestow His guidance upon people who disbelieved after their belief and had witnessed that the Messenger is indeed the truth' (3:86). 'And what is beyond truth except misguidance?' (10:86). Thus, for the captive, sooner or later his fate is freedom either as an act of grace or in exchange for ransom that is pledged by him or his family, as mentioned in the noble verse regarding mandatory interaction with captives.

In light of what has been discussed, let us see what is found in the books of Hadith,[19] if they agree with what is found in the book of Allah (SWT), and whether they are in harmony with the Mohammedan path—the path which is recommended by the Qur'an regarding war and captives.

We read in the Musnad of Ahmad ibn Hanbal,[20] on the authority of Ibn Abbas, who said that Umar bin al-Khattab said:

---

[18] As mentioned in a Hadith of Aisha.

[19] Sahih Muslim (1763), Sunan al-Tirmidhi (3081), Sunan Abi Dawod (2690), Musnad Ahmad (1/31 and 1/33).

[20] Ahmad ibn Hanbal is one of the six books deemed to be of high authenticity amongst Sunni Muslims.

On the day of the battle of Badr . . . Allah defeated the polytheists, and seventy men from them were killed and seventy were made captive. The Prophet (PBUH) then sought the advice of Abu Bakr, Ali and Umar (may Allah be pleased with them). Abu Bakr responded saying; 'Oh Prophet of Allah (SWT), these people are the children of our uncles, our kinsfolk and our brothers. It is my opinion, that you may take from them ransom which will strengthen us against the disbelievers, and perhaps Allah (SWT) will guide them and support us through them.' The Prophet (PBUH) responded, saying: 'what is your opinion oh son of Al-Khattab?' I replied; 'By Allah, I do not concur with Abu Bakr. My position is that you permit me to behead this person (a family member of Umar's). And that you permit Ali (RA) to execute Uqayl (His brother) and Hamzah to execute his brother.[21] This, so that Allah may know that there is no leniency in our hearts for the polytheists; these are their champions, their leaders and their commanders.' The Prophet (PBUH) inclined towards the position of Abu Bakr, and not to mine, and thus took from them ransom. The following day I set off in the morning to meet the Prophet (PBUH). I found him and Abu Bakr both seated and weeping, and said to them; 'Oh Messenger of Allah, what has caused you and your companion to weep? Tell me so that if I find a reason to weep I shall weep, and if I find no reason to, then I shall feign weeping for your weeping.' The Prophet (PBUH) replied; 'Due to the suggestion of your companions regarding ransom, your punishment was shown to me closer than this tree to a neighbouring one'; then Allah revealed: 'It is not for a Prophet to take captives until he has sufficiently suppressed the enemies in the land . . .' up to His saying: 'If not for a decree from Allah that preceded, you would have been touched for what you took . . .' (8:67), of ransom; thereafter Allah made spoils of war lawful for them. On the day of the battle of Uhud,

---

[21]   Al-Abbas.

the following year, they were punished for what they did on the day of Badr by taking the ransom; hence, seventy of them were killed and the companions of the Prophet (PBUH) fled and left him; and his front tooth was broken, his helmet was cracked, and blood flowed upon his face. Thereafter, Allah revealed: 'And when a calamity befell you after you had inflicted twice as much [on your foes], you said, "How has this come about?" Say: "It has come from your own selves . . ." (3:165) because you have taken the ransom.'[22]

The Hadith mentions that Umar bin al-Khattab suggested to the Prophet (PBUH) to kill the captives. This position is not accepted by Allah (SWT) in His book, nor is it accepted by the Prophet (PBUH) in his tradition or his legislation. The Prophet (PBUH) is the most knowledgeable of creation regarding Allah (SWT) and regarding His book and how to preach the message in which manner in each context; he does not follow anything except what is revealed to him by Allah (SWT). It is against his nature to follow inclinations. Moreover, killing the captives does not negate the reality that they were captives before killing them! Neither is killing the captives after war 'vanquishing the enemy' since vanquishing the enemy is to achieve victory and control in the battlefield before taking captives. 'Until you have vanquished them, then bind them [as captives] firmly' (47:4). This is not after taking them as captives.

The divine admonition was directed towards haste in taking captives and not in the cessation of killing them after taking them as captives. There is no indication in the verse to kill the captives or to take captives before vanquishing the enemy. The instruction and guidance of the Prophet (PBUH) to his soldiers was not to bring him captives either; in fact, it was this taking of the captives which was the reason for the admonition from Allah (SWT) in the verse.

As to those whom Umar advised to be killed (claiming them to be their champions, their leaders, and their commanders), we find that

---

[22] Musnad Ahmad.

amongst them was al-Abbas, whom the Prophet (PBUH), before the battle, ordered not be killed perhaps due the knowledge of the Prophet (PBUH) that al-Abbas was concealing his Islam. Despite this, the actions of the Prophet (PBUH) do not need us to provide a pretext; rather we should accept them with total obedience and complete submission, as per the statement of Allah (SWT): 'And accept in willing submission' (33:56). Also amongst them was Uquayl, the brother of Ali bin Abi Talib (AS).

Are these the champions of the disbelievers, their leaders, and their commanders? These are the descendants of Hashim,[23] the uncle of the Prophet (PBUH), and his cousin. Umar desired, as mentioned in the Hadith, that Hamza (RA) embark upon killing his brother al-Abbas, whom the Prophet forbade the soldiers from killing, which was known to Umar, and that Ali (AS) kill his brother Uqayl (RA). And yet another man Umar would kill by himself (the Hadith fails to mention his name). Were these all the captives of Badr? Why does the Hadith limit the number to these three? Is the killing of these three people mercy, which the Prophet of mercy (PBUH) came with?

They want to make apparent in the Hadith the desire of Umar bin al-Khattab to kill the polytheists, as per his statement: 'This, so that Allah (SWT) may know that there is no leniency in our hearts for the polytheists; these are their champions, their leaders and their commanders.' This statement is inadmissible since the desire to kill the disbelievers should be in war, not after taking captives. Indeed, we clarified the method of interacting with captives in Islam. As for the knowledge of Allah (SWT) regarding what is in their hearts, there is no requirement for anyone to make this apparent by manifest actions since Allah (SWT) says that 'he is Knowing of the (inmost secrets) of the hearts' (11:5).

The statement 'Their champions, their leaders and their commanders' is incorrect since they were not! It is not mentioned in any of the sources of Islam that al-Abbas and Uqayl (RA) were from the leaders of disbelief, their champions, and their commanders. And what about

---

23   The clan of the Prophet (PBUH).

the rest of the seventy captives? And why is the Hadith confined to the descendants of Hashim in names, and why was the third person's name omitted? Furthermore, where is the opinion of Ali bin Abi Talib, who is mentioned in the Hadith, as being one whom the Prophet sought advice from, just as Abu Bakr and Umar? Why is it not mentioned?

The Hadith is focused on assuming the soundness of the opinion of Umar bin al-Khattab in killing the captives, which is in contrast to the action of the Prophet (PBUH) in not killing them! In fact, it destroys the Prophet's legislation of war in Islam regarding the method of interaction with captives, and it contradicts the book of Allah (SWT) and the tradition of the honourable Messenger (PBUH). The matter doesn't end here; indeed, it goes further to show that the conduct of the infallible Messenger and his legislation in treatment of the captives was a mistake that he was accountable for, as if there is an equal legislator with him who is able to fulfil the message correctly whilst the Prophet (PBUH) misses the mark in its fulfilment!

The Hadith portrays the Prophet (PBUH) as being remorseful for going against the opinion of Umar and accepting ransom from the captives and continuing to weep for this reason. Umar said to him when he found him weeping, 'Oh Messenger of Allah (SWT), what has caused you and your companion to weep? Tell me so that if I find a reason to weep I shall weep, and if I find no reason to, then I shall feign weeping for your weeping.' This implies that the weeping of the Prophet (PBUH) is perhaps without reason or for something unnecessary; and if this is the case, then the weeping is for show or in vain. Can this be attributed to the Prophet (PBUH)? Indeed, the statement of Umar is this: 'If I find a reason to weep I shall weep, and if I find no reason . . .' He doubts the sincerity of the Prophet's weeping and his actions and offers to shed crocodile tears for the weeping of the Messenger and his companion out of courtesy for them despite being unconvinced as to the reason of their weeping. 'If I find no reason to, than I shall feign weeping for your weeping.'

This manner of questioning the Messenger of Allah (PBUH)—'What has caused you and your companion to weep?'—is not in agreement with admiration of his noble person. The Prophet (PBUH) said in response to Umar, 'Your punishment has appeared to me closer than the proximity of this tree.' The phrase *to a tree nearby* is absolutely not the Prophet's; neither is what follows. Did the infallible Messenger (PBUH) act in contrary to the command of Allah (SWT) so He punished him for his conduct?[24] The Hadith continues and says, 'Then Allah (SWT) revealed: "It is not for a Prophet to take captives until he has sufficiently suppressed the enemies in the land . . .", up to His saying; "If not for a decree from Allah that preceded, you would have been touched for what you took . . ." (8:68), of ransom.' What is apparent from this section of Hadith, which is definitely not the words of the Messenger (PBUH), is the attribution of blame to the infallible Prophet because of his acceptance of ransom and the accusation of failure in correctly fulfilling the message! This, in fact, is the entire purpose of the Hadith.

What is known is that ransom is either agreed upon with the captive or imposed upon him; in turn, he forfeits it from his wealth at home, or his benefactors may pay it on his behalf. It is not expected for the captive to have anything with him except his bare skin. Yet what is noticeable from the Hadith is the presumption that the ransom money was already with the captives and that the Prophet seized it from them and that the next day he wept due to this! It is mentioned in the Hadith: 'The Prophet (PBUH) inclined towards the position of Abu Bakr, and not to mine, and thus he took from them the ransom. The following day I set off to meet the Prophet (PBUH). I found him and Abu Bakr both seated and weeping.' Yet the captive has absolutely nothing except for an agreement of the type of ransom to be paid and its amount. The ransom may also be a certain task that the captive should do. In the case of some of these captives, the ransom was simply an agreement to teach a number of children![25] It cannot be said that the Prophet (PBUH) seized the ransom since the captives had nothing with them. The only thing that could be said perhaps is that he accepted the ransom that should be paid subsequently; thus, the statement 'He took from them ransom' is erroneous in the first place.

---

24   'They were punished for what they have done on the day of Badr.'
25   Musnad Ahmad.

The most credible commentary on the verse, 'You would have been touched for what you took', is either 'what you took' as captives from the enemy before vanquishing them (since it was not fitting for them to take captives before vanquishing the enemy) or 'what you took' from the transient wealth of this world, which was with the captives, from war materials to possessions. This is war booty, since what succeeds the verse is 'Enjoy, then, all that which you have captured (of booty)—for it is lawful and clean—and remain conscious of Allah. Surely Allah is Ever Forgiving, Most Merciful' (8:69). In both cases, the blame is placed on the companions and not upon the Prophet (PBUH) since it is impossible to lay blame upon him due to the guideline of Allah (SWT): 'So turn away from them; you are never to be blamed' (51:54).

The Hadith continues: 'Thereafter Allah (SWT) made spoils of war lawful.' In fact, war booty was the reason for the divine reprimand regarding the haste in taking captives since they are *gains of the world*. 'Had there not been a previous decree from Allah', had not the mercy of Allah (SWT) preceded His anger, the punishment and retribution descending upon them would have been inescapable. 'A stern punishment would have afflicted you for what you had taken', but 'Allah will never chastise them while you are amongst them' (8:33). Allah (SWT) has indeed taken a covenant upon himself not to punish a people if amongst them is the Messenger of Allah (PBUH) since amongst them may be those in whose hearts Muhammad is present by love more than their parents and children. Thus the mercy, personified by Muhammad (PBUH), the Prophet of mercy, embraces them; hence, Allah (SWT) permits for them the acquisition of the spoils of war for his sake when it was not permitted for any previous Prophet. 'Enjoy, then, all that which you have captured (of booty)—for it is lawful and clean—and remain conscious of Allah' (8:69).

As for the taking of ransom from the captives, Allah (SWT) has clarified in His revelation: 'Thereafter [you are entitled to] set them free, either by an act of grace, or against ransom' (4:74). Ransom is not war booty. Since the verses in question refer to the taking of war booty and not to the acceptance of ransom, then there is no room for criticising acceptance of ransom from the captives, and the Prophet

(PBUH) did as Allah (SWT) commanded him, as in the above verse. Anything other than this position categorically contradicts the clear verses of the Qur'an and the confirmed practice of the Prophet (PBUH).

Thus, the disapproval and censure were placed upon the companions for their haste in taking captives for war booty and not upon the Prophet (PBUH) for his interaction with the captives in accordance with what was revealed to him in accepting ransom. So the Muslim should be aware of his standing in relation to the infallible Prophet (PBUH)! Let us read the verses mentioned in the Hadith sequentially to make clear that the censure is laid upon the companions for their haste in taking captives to gain war booty and not upon the Prophet (PBUH) for his acceptance of ransom.

Allah (SWT) says: 'It is not for a Prophet to take captives until he has sufficiently suppressed the enemies in the land. You [plural] seek the gains of the world whereas Allah desires [for you the bounties of] the Hereafter. Allah is All-Mighty, All-Wise. If not for a decree from Allah that preceded, you [plural] would have been touched for what you [plural] took by a great punishment. Enjoy, then, all that which you [plural] have captured [of booty]—for it is lawful and clean—and remain conscious of Allah, indeed, Allah is Most Forgiving, Most Merciful' (8:67–69).

As for the verses that immediately follow, they address the Messenger (PBUH) in relation to the captives that were brought to him by the soldiers. Allah (SWT) said, 'O Prophet! Say to those captives in your [plural] hands: 'If it is known to Allah there is goodness in your hearts, He will give you that which is better than what has been taken away from you [i.e. of war booty] . . . and He will forgive you. Allah is Ever Forgiving, Most Merciful. But if they seek to betray you [O Muhammad], know that they had already betrayed Allah. Therefore He made you prevail over them. Allah is All-Knowing, All-Wise' (8:70–71).

These verses clarify the manner of interaction with captives, which is addressing them and receiving them with the mercy that they hadn't known before and consoling them by way of inviting them to goodness and righteousness so that Allah (SWT) may forgive them. 'If Allah finds any goodness in your hearts, He will give you that which is better than what has been taken from you.' This invitation came after what had been taken away from the captives to reform their consciences so that Allah (SWT) may give them better than what they had lost. Indeed, the Prophet of mercy was sent to perfect moral character. And if they consented, they would receive sustenance better than what was taken from them of war booty; moreover, they would be forgiven. 'And He will forgive you. Allah is Most Forgiving, Most Merciful.' Allah (SWT) clarified for his noble Prophet (PBUH) that the liberation of the captives is what should happen even if they have intentions of evil and betrayal. Moreover, their ill intentions must not be the reason for preventing their release; indeed, Allah (SWT) is the guarantor of His Prophet's safety. Nor shall their betrayal help them to escape if they do so. 'But if they seek to betray you, know that they had already betrayed Allah and He made you prevail over them' (8:71). These are the verses that relate to the captives, and indeed, the divine speech was directed at the Prophet (PBUH) that he should follow what is revealed to him.

I am astonished at those who want to place Umar (RA) in positions like these and then say that they are of his virtues! Is it virtuous to contradict the infallible Messenger and the book of Allah, the All-Wise? It seems to me that there is a trend found in certain ahadith which sanctions disrespect of the actions of the Messenger (PBUH) and subsequently approves the contradicting position, thus finding fault with the Prophet (PBUH) so that there remains no sanctity for his actions, views, or his noble person; and these are all attributed to Umar bin al-Khattab (RA) and mentioned as his virtue! In fact, there is nothing worse than depicting a companion as someone who contradicts the Messenger of Allah (PBUH) since it negates his companionship; moreover, it negates his Islam in one stroke. The divine command for the believers is to 'accept in willing submission' (4:65) the way, guidance, and judgement of the Prophet (PBUH).

These types of ahadith, even if presented in the form of praise for Umar (RA), demonstrating his strength and power, in reality disparages him and attributes to him disobedience and ill temper. What is more, it violates the infallibility of the Prophet (PBUH) and the sanctity of his actions, commands, and noble person, which Allah (SWT) has ordained upon the believers in His law:

> So whatever the Messenger consigns unto you, take it, and from whatever he forbids you from, abstain. (59:7)

> Whoever obeys the Messenger, has indeed obeyed Allah. (4:80)

> Beware! Those who go against his [Messenger's] order lest a trial or severe punishment afflict them. (24:63)

> So that you may believe in Allah and His Messenger, and support him, and revere him, and celebrate his glory, morning and evening. (48:9)

> Oh you who came to believe, obey Allah and obey the Messenger and do not cause your deeds to be nullified. (47:33)

Thus, the Hadith does not establish any principle of Islamic jurisprudence; rather, it violates the God-given principles of human rights in relation to captives as well as the ethical management of war in Islam. The combatants are required not to hasten in taking captives from the enemy, except after vanquishing them, and to not continue killing them after this. Thus, the Hadith has no legislative importance regarding captives, with the exception of illustrating the contradiction of Umar with the action of the Prophet (PBUH) and then the attempt to demonstrate the correctness of this contradiction in such a way that the action of the Prophet (PBUH) is deemed incorrect!

I do not believe that there is a companion who would rejoice if he is described as being in conflict with the Prophet (PBUH)! It is impossible that correctness be in conflict with the Prophet (PBUH). Moreover, there is a clear contradiction in the Hadith with the book of Allah (SWT) regarding what is attributed to Umar bin al-Khattab

(RA). Allah (SWT) states regarding the captives, 'Thereafter set them free, either by an act of grace, or against ransom' (47:33), whereas Umar calls for the killing of the captives!

It is written that the Prophet (PBUH) ordered before the beginning of the war, 'Whoever amongst you meets Al-Abbas should not fight him; indeed he was forced to come to war.'[26] Is it mentioned that Umar (RA) did not hear the directive of the Messenger, the leader of his army before the battle? It is basic knowledge that every word that is issued from the commander before the battle is heeded, respected, and pursued by all the soldiers, let alone the fact that the commander in this case is the Prophet and the Messenger. If there had been a preceding order from the Messenger (PBUH) not to kill al-Abbas in the battlefield, how can it then be said that Umar (RA) insisted upon the killing of al-Abbas after he was taken as a captive?

As mentioned earlier, the purpose of the Hadith is to illustrate the correctness of the opinion of Umar in contrast to the action of the Prophet (PBUH)! However, history testified against this and proved that the taking of ransom was the correct position. Umar, during his reign, was in need of al-Abbas (RA), whom he previously wanted killed, to supplicate through him[27] to Allah (SWT) for rain and hence save the people from drought! Is there a more correct position other than what was done by the Prophet (PBUH) in accepting ransom? This is not intended as an evidence of correctness; rather, correctness is based on what Allah (SWT) commanded and on what was implemented by the Prophet (PBUH).

It is mentioned in another Hadith that Umar went too far in the shackling of al-Abbas after his capture, which caused him to groan all night, and that the Prophet (PBUH) was unable to sleep from the groaning of his uncle. 'On the authority of Ibn Aaidh, that Umar, after the shackling of the chains of the captives, tightened the chains of Al-Abbas; the Messenger (PBUH) heard him groaning and was unable

---

[26]   Mustadrak Ala Sahihayn.

[27]   Salat Ul Istisqaa.

to sleep.'[28] Is what is meant to be understood from this that Umar had something in his heart against the singling out of al-Abbas by the Prophet (PBUH) in his guideline 'Whoever amongst you meets Al-Abbas should not fight him, indeed he was forced to come to war'? Even if we suppose that Umar did not hear from the Prophet (PBUH) the imperative of avoiding al-Abbas in the battlefield, wasn't there anyone who had heard and mentioned this to Umar? Furthermore, is it not that this action is such a distress to the Prophet (PBUH) that it prevented him from sleeping? Moreover, is it not the intention to include Umar in the verse 'Those who hurt the Messenger of Allah— for them is a painful punishment'? (9:61).

The Hadith goes further and includes the Battle of Uhud, stating, 'On the battle of Uhud, the following year they were punished for taking the ransom on the day of Badr.'[29] What is meant by 'were punished' here is the Prophet (PBUH) since it is he who took ransom as mentioned in the Hadith! The verb used is in the passive plural form so as to conceal the enormity of the statement—a statement that every Muslim would be embarrassed to utter upon his lips or allow to cross his mind; that is, the Prophet (PBUH) was punished for what he did on the day of Badr of taking ransom. 'And his front tooth was broken, his helmet was smashed on his head, and blood flowed upon his face and his companions fled and left him.'

This is a statement akin to gloating over the Prophet (PBUH) since he embraced the opinion of Abu Bakr (RA) and did not consider the opinion of Umar, who said, 'He did not incline towards my position.' The Hadith says, 'The Prophet (PBUH) inclined towards the position of Abu Bakr, and not to mine, and thus took from them ransom.' The Messenger (PBUH) does not follow personal inclination; rather, he follows what is revealed to him. Allah (SWT) says, '[Oh Muhammad tell them] I only act upon what is revealed to me' (46:9). Yet the Hadith states that the Prophet (PBUH) follows his inclinations! Is this the way of Umar bin al-Khattab (RA), the second caliph?

---

[28] Fath Al Bari.
[29] Musnad Ahmad.

As we have mentioned earlier, the reason for the defeat of the companions in the Battle of Uhud was their violation and disobedience of the Prophet's (PBUH) order and their abandonment of their posts, not the acceptance of ransom from the captives by the Prophet (PBUH) in the Battle of Badr in the previous year, as commanded by Allah (SWT). In fact, the punishment and sufferance are solely due to disobeying the order of the Prophet (PBUH) since obeying him is obeying Allah (SWT), and for this reason, the divine warning from his disobedience is conveyed. 'Let those who dissent from the Prophet's order, beware, lest a trial or severe punishment befalls them' (24:63).

Thus, the defeat of the companions in the Battle of Uhud was the consequence of disobeying the Prophet's command, which Allah (SWT) warned against. The command of the Messenger should be obeyed categorically without hesitation since obeying the Messenger is inseparable from obeying Allah (SWT), hence His saying, 'He who obeys the Messenger has indeed obeyed Allah' (4:80). The Qur'anic verse that is mentioned in the Hadith indicates this unequivocally when it is read in its entirety: 'And how come when a calamity befell you, after you had inflicted twice as much [on your foes], you [plural] said, "From where is this?" Say [O Muhammad], "It is from your own selves." Indeed, Allah is over all things competent' (3:165).

The divine address is directed at those that wondered, 'From where is this?' It is beyond the Messenger of Allah (PBUH) from being baffled with regard to why Allah (SWT) would afflict them, saying to his Lord, 'From where is this?' Thus, the questioning is from the companions, who were expecting the divine support, as occurred in the Battle of Badr. It appears from the wording that this question was directed at the Messenger (PBUH), the guide (PBUH), as if they were enquiring about the divine intervention for their support since they were battling disbelievers to support the religion of Muhammed (PBUH).

The divine response regarding their question was given: 'Say [O Muhammad], "It is from your own selves . . ."' It was due to their disobedience of the Prophet's command and abandoning their posts, because disobedience to the Prophet (PBUH) is in fact disobedience to Allah (SWT). 'And you disobeyed [the Prophet] after He showed you what you intensely desire' (3:152). There is no divine support in disobeying the Prophet even if the enemy is a disbeliever! Moreover, the disobeying of the Prophet's commands here was for gaining booty when they witnessed the first signs of their victory and the defeat of the polytheists. They abandoned their positions, which the Prophet (PBUH) commanded against,[30] and for the second time, they desired 'the gains of this world, whereas Allah desires the Hereafter' (8:67). Allah (SWT) says, 'Some of you desired this world and some of you desired the hereafter' (3:152).

Disobedience of the Prophet's command comes with it the unavoidable consequence of punishment. 'Let those who dissent from the Prophet's order, beware, lest a trial or severe punishment befalls them' (24:63). Then how could they hope for support from Allah (SWT) and ask 'From where is this?' whilst they went against the command of their Prophet despite the warning of Allah (SWT)? Therefore, Allah (SWT) said, 'Say, "It is from your own selves."' This is the divine answer to their question about their defeat in the Battle of Uhud for them, and every discerning believer who hopes for Allah (SWT) and the hereafter, to know that the obedience of the Prophet's command is more important than fighting disbelievers and polytheists and defeating them in the battlefield and that victory will never be achieved whilst disobeying him!

How then can the disobeying of the Prophet's command by the companions, the combatants, be overlooked when it is a major sin that obligates calamity and severe punishment? This was the direct reason for their defeat in the Battle of Uhud. How can it be justified to say that the acceptance of ransom by the Prophet (PBUH) from the captives in the Battle of Badr—in the previous year—and his dissension from the view of Umar are the direct reasons for the defeat

---

[30] As the Hadith says: 'Even if you see us being snatched by birds of prey, do not abandon your posts, until you are discharged. And if you see us defeating the enemy and have vanquished them, do not abandon your posts, until you are discharged!'

of the companions in the Battle of Uhud? I say *defeat of the companions* because the Prophet (PBUH) was never defeated; he (PBUH) never retreated from his position in the battlefield even by a single step. It is narrated that Ali (AS) said, 'When fear of fighting becomes fiery and the two factions engage [in fighting], we used to seek protection with the Messenger of Allah (SWT) (PBUH); no one would be closer to the enemy than he.'[31] Indeed, he persisted steadfast, unsurpassed, exceeding the firm mountains, calling out to them from their rear, and they were fleeing without casting even a side glance at anyone. Allah (SWT) describes them thus: 'Recall when you were fleeing without casting even a side glance at anyone, and the Messenger was calling out to you from your rear' (3:152).

Yielding is not a character trait that befits the infallible Messenger of Allah (PBUH), the possessor of perfect character, nor is it appropriate to attribute it to him. Under no circumstances is it acceptable to say that the action of the Prophet (PBUH) in the Battle of Badr was the reason for the defeat in the Battle of Uhud so as to overlook the dissension of the companions in their lack of commitment and reverence and, more seriously, their disobedience of the command of the noble Prophet (PBUH)—which Allah (SWT) confirmed in His revelation: 'And you disobeyed [the Prophet] after He showed you what you intensely desire' (3:152)—and to cast the blame upon the greatest infallible Messenger for his dissension with the view of Umar, challenging the soundness of his action in following his Lord's revelation that Allah (SWT) himself confirmed in His noble book: 'Tell them oh Muhammad . . . I only act upon what is revealed to me' (46:9).

This statement in the Hadith, 'The companions of the Prophet (PBUH) fled and left him,' which ascribes to the companions' defeat and desertion in the battlefield, needs questioning because it shows that the narrator to whom the Hadith is attributed was not among the companions of the Prophet (PBUH) who fought in the Battle of Uhud but was an observer from a distance; otherwise, he'd also be among those who took flight! The synopsis of the Hadith is that

---

[31]   Musnad Ahmed.

the alleged *punishment of the Prophet* on the day of Uhud[32] was due to his opposition of the view of Umar and the taking of ransom in the Battle of Badr the year before; that his weeping at the time did not bring salvation for him; in addition, that the opinion of Umar was better than the action of the greatest Prophet (PBUH) and that Allah (SWT) backed Umar and condemned His Prophet whom He sent! At the same time, it disregards the disobedience of the archers and their violation of the command of the Prophet (PBUH), which Allah (SWT) confirmed in His book: 'And you disobeyed (the Prophet) after He showed you what you intensely desire' (3:152). They abandoned their posts that the Prophet (PBUH) ordered them to remain at even if they were snatched by raptors! This is the unequivocal reason for their defeat in the Battle of Uhud since the lack of obedience to the Prophet (PBUH) is direct disobedience to Allah (SWT)!

Is this the intended lesson that is to be learned by the Muslims from the Battle of Badr—that the disobedience to the Prophet (PBUH) of a companion necessitates his punishment and defeat? And the dissension of the companions of the Prophet, and hence Allah (SWT), the Hadith remains quiet about, so it is viewed as innocuous and of no consequence on what took place! Has not the time come to examine these types of ahadith? Does not the prohibition of critical reading of Islamic sources to check the likes of these ahadith include us amongst those addressed in the saying of Allah (SWT): 'When it is said to them "Follow what Allah has revealed," they say: "Rather we will follow what we found our forefathers following"' (31:21)?

Is it not more appropriate to depict the companions (RA) as the most obedient of people for the Prophet (PBUH), which Allah (SWT) obligated upon them, instead of attributing to one of them disobedience and attempting to justify this? Would a companion be commended for his obedience to the Prophet (PBUH) or for disobeying him? Is what is intended from the episode of the captives of Badr anything other than to establish blame upon the best of

---

[32] 'His front tooth was broken, his helmet was smashed on his head, and blood flowed upon his face; and his companions deserted him.'

humanity? Is this the path of salvation unto Allah (SWT) on the day of resurrection?

'Thus We do clarify the Verses of revelation so that the way of those who are lost in sin might become distinct' (6:55).

10

The Accusation of Being Accompanied by the Devil

Allah (SWT) says, 'And whoever is blinded from remembrance of the Most Merciful—we assign to him a devil as a companion for him' (43:36).

Allah (SWT) also says, 'And he to whom Satan is a companion, what an evil companion' (4:38).

A devil is an assigned companion for the one who is blinded from remembrance of the Most Merciful; the devil embraces the world as his sole purpose and goal, coveting its finery and temptations, contrary to the intelligent, who controls his ego and devotes his life to the preparation of death and who places the hereafter before his eyes, substituting the life of this world. It is he who stands in prayer at the dead of night for his Lord, fasts the day for intimacy, and wanders in His love. It is he whom the Qur'an describes thus: 'Their sides forsake their beds' (32:16). It is he whom Allah (SWT) accounts as 'And the servants of the Most Merciful are those who walk upon the earth gently, and when the ignorant address them, they respond with "peace"' (25:63).

They are the ones who are praised by their Lord in His clear revelation for their noble attributes, whose hearts have become occupied with the awareness of Allah (SWT), and who have committed themselves to the proximity of the truthful *awliyaa*[1] due to the obligation of the command of Allah (SWT) for them. Their Lord refined them, saying, 'Be conscious of Allah and accompany the truthful ones' (9:119). The truthful ones are the people of attachment with the messenger of Allah (PBUH), displaying faith in their Lord and pursuing His pleasure by praying throughout the night and fasting throughout the day, avoiding His prohibitions and fleeing towards Him in keeping with His statement: 'So flee to Allah' (51:50). He dressed them with the attribute of servanthood and adorned them with being conscious of Him. They are the righteous servants of Allah (SWT), and this entitles them as the truthful ones, who have true faith in the messenger of Allah (PBUH): 'And they witness that the Messenger is truth' (3:86).

Thus, the people of faith in Allah (SWT), if they are garbed with God consciousness, become the closest of peoples to having faith in the messenger of Allah (PBUH). 'O you who have come to believe, be conscious of Allah and have faith in His Messenger; He will give you a double portion of His mercy and assign for you a light by which you will walk and forgive you' (57:28). And hence they become the elite servants of Allah (SWT), the beloveds of the Prophet (PBUH), who said in their regard, '"I desire to meet my brothers." It was said to him: "Are we not your brothers?" He replied: "You are my companions. My brothers are those who believe in me having never seen me."'[2]

They are the people of faith in Allah (SWT), whose hearts are replete with His awareness; the divine dialogue is directed at them, inciting them to the station of the truthful ones, the people with faith in the Messenger of Allah (PBUH). They have reached the most radiant station. 'They will not be grieved by the greatest terror, and they will be welcomed by the angels' (21:103). It is they who have attained what Allah (SWT) has promised. 'O you who have come to believe,

---

[1]   Awliyaa: the saintly people amongst the umma.

[2]   Musnad Ahmed.

be conscious of Allah and have faith in His Messenger; He will give
you a double portion of His mercy and assign for you a light by which
you will walk and forgive you, and Allah is the most Forgiving, most
Merciful' (57:28).

To this group, the devil has no access since they are the sincere
servants of Allah (SWT), His elite, whom He describes as 'Verily, My
servants—no authority will you [Devil] have over them' (15:42). He
also says: 'Allah favours with His mercy whoever He wills' (2:105).
Thus, those who believe in Allah (SWT), are conscious of Him, and
believe in His Messenger (PBUH), He has safeguarded them from the
company of the devil explicitly in the Qur'an. 'Indeed, he [the Devil]
has no authority over those who have come to believe and depend
on their Lord. His authority is only over those who ally themselves
with him and those who ascribe to him a share in God's divinity'
(16:99–100). It is possible for one who belongs to this group to reach
such an elevated status of the soul that the divine truth becomes his
hearing, his sight, his hand, his leg, and his faculties,[3] and therefore
he utters nothing but truth, like the statement of Bastami (RH):
'Glory be to me, how great my affair.' This statement was not rejected
by Ibn Qayyim Aljawziyyah[4] nor Ibn Taymiyyah al-Harrani,[5] who

---

[3]   On the authority of Abu Hurayrah (may Allah be pleased with him),
       who said that the Messenger of Allah (PHUH) said, 'Allah (mighty
       and sublime be he) said, "Whosoever shows enmity to someone
       devoted to me, I shall be at war with him. My servant draws not near
       to me with anything more loved by me than the religious duties I have
       enjoined upon him, and my servant continues to draw near to me with
       supererogatory works so that I shall love him. When I love him, I am
       his hearing with which he hears, his seeing with which he sees, his hand
       with which he works, and his foot with which he walks. Were he to ask
       [something] of me, I would surely give it to him, and were he to ask me
       for refuge, I would surely grant him it. I do not hesitate about anything
       as much as I hesitate about [seizing] the soul of my faithful servant: he
       hates death, and I hate hurting him."' It was related by al-Bukhari.
[4]   Ibn Qayyim: an Islamic jurist and theologian.
[5]   Ibn Taymiyyah: An Islamic jurist and theologian and teacher of Ibn
       Qayyim.

is considered by many of those who take him as an imam to be in opposition to those who follow this sacred path of divine cognisance.

If all sides attest to the spiritual elevation of this group, and *thus their protection* against the devil as a companion, then how do they presume that the Messenger of Allah (PBUH), whom He chose from amongst them and sent to teach them revelation and wisdom so that they'd know the path to Allah (SWT) and how to draw near to Him, had a devil as a companion which became Muslim and that it ordered him only to do good? Owing to the fact that this Hadith appears in Sahih Muslim, is it compulsory upon us to accept it? Is it forbidden to reject anything from Sahih Muslim even if it diminishes the noble status of the Messenger (PBUH)? It is said that it is the most authentic book after the book of Allah—without evidence—and that if one rejects it, they have destroyed the Sunnah!

Do they not see that if one accepts it entirely, they have destroyed their faith and religion in its entirety? What is more, one would make the status of the Prophet (PBUH) less than that of one of the scholars! How would a Muslim respond if it is said to him or her that one of the Gnostic scholars—like Abdul Qadir al-Jaylani,[6] ar-Rifai', al-Badawi, al-Shadhili, and at-Tijani (RA)—had a companion who was a disbelieving devil and that this is because according to the Hadith, the only devil that converted to Islam was that of the Prophet (PBUH)? We seek refuge in you, O Allah (SWT), from the mention of this statement even if it be in an effort to display its wickedness. Indeed, you are fully aware of our intentions and what is hidden in our breasts; there is no strength or power except through you.

What remains of the religion for the one who states that the Prophet (PBUH) has a Muslim devil who commands him? Consequently, it becomes incumbent upon anyone who accepts this as faith to state that everybody, including Abu Bakr and Umar, have disbelieving devils as companions who command them with evil since the good command is specifically for the Prophet (PBUH), as mentioned. What is more

---

6   Abdul Qadir: Hanbali jurist and Sufi from Baghdad. The Qadiriyya was his patronym.

shocking than this position is the people's acceptance of the ahadith that prefers Umar over the Prophet (PBUH) due to the support of Allah (SWT) for Umar rather than the Prophet (PBUH) when they differed, as mentioned regarding the context of the captives of Badr; in other words, Allah (SWT) preferred one who had a devil as a companion that commanded him with evil!

It may be said that the devil of Abu Bakr and Umar is not necessarily a disbelieving one since there is no evidence against it. This position is faced with the opposite—i.e. there is no evidence for or against it, in which case the soundest position is one of doubt regarding the Islam of both their devils. On the other hand, regarding the devil of Aisha (RA), there is explicit text confirming that it did not become Muslim, which means she had a disbelieving devil companion, different to the companion (devil) of the Messenger of Allah (PBUH)! Otherwise, there would have been no room for criticism levelled against her due to her devil if it was not different to the supposed devil of the Messenger (PBUH). There is no power or strength save in Allah! Indeed, this statement is attributed to Abu Bakr (RA): 'Verily, I have a devil that comes near unto me!'[7]

How is this Hadith consistent with these statements of Allah (SWT): 'Verily, My servants—no authority will you have over them' (15:42) and 'Indeed, he has no authority over those who have come to believe and depend on their Lord' (16:99). It is also consistent with the confirmation of Satan in the Qur'an: '[None will be safe from me] except, Your sincere servants from among them' (15:40). These verses were aimed particularly at those to whom the Prophet (PBUH) was sent. Can it be that he (PBUH) in the sight of Allah (SWT) is lower than them in station since he had a devil which converted to Islam due to the help of Allah (SWT)?

It is mentioned in Sahih Muslim:

> Aisha (RA) the wife of messenger (PBUH), reported that one day Allah's Messenger (PBUH) went out of her

---

[7]   Majma' az-Zawaid Lil-Haythami.

[apartment] during the night and she felt jealous. He then returned seeing her [in this agitated state of mind]. He said: 'Aisha, what has happened to you? Do you feel jealous?' Thereupon she replied: 'How can it be that one like me should not feel jealous in regard to one like you?' Thereupon the Prophet (PBUH) said: 'did your devil come to you?', she replied: 'Oh messenger of Allah (SWT), do I have a devil?' He said: 'Yes', so she asked: 'does everyone have a devil?' He said: 'Yes'. She again asked: 'do you likewise have a devil oh messenger of Allah?' He said: 'Yes, but my Lord has helped me against him until he has become Muslim.'[8]

In a similar Hadith, the Prophet (PBUH) said:

'There is none from amongst you who does not have a companion from the Jinn.' The companions asked: 'Do you likewise oh messenger of Allah (SWT)?' Thereupon he said: 'Yes, but Allah helped me against him, it has become Muslim and does not command me except with good.'[9]

Also in the Musnad of Imam Ahmad, it is reported that the Prophet (PBUH) said to his companions:

'Don't enter the chambers of women whose husbands are absent, since the devil flows in you like the flowing of blood.' We replied: 'and in you too, Oh messenger of Allah (SWT), do you have a devil?' He said: 'Yes, but my Lord has helped me against him, so it has become Muslim.'[10]

It is known from the text of the Qur'an that the devil is a disbeliever. 'And Sulaiman did not disbelieve but the devils disbelieved' (2:102). Regarding the jinn, Allah (SWT) says, 'And amongst us (Jinn) are the righteous, and others that are not so' (72:11). He (SWT) also

---

8   Sahih Muslim.
9   Sahih Muslim.
10   Musnad Ahmad.

mentions, 'And amongst us are Muslims, as well as the unjust' (72:14). Therefore, the one who believes this Hadith has to accept that the disbeliever from amongst the jinn is the devil companion. And what can be deemed from the above ahadith is that—if accepted—Abu Bakr (RA), Umar (RA), Aisha (RA), and the rest of the companions of the Prophet (PBUH), each of them has a disbelieving devil companion who commands the doing of evil! Such a person should also believe that the Prophet (PBUH) is influenced in the undertaking of good by either a devil who accepted Islam or Allah (SWT)! It can therefore be possible to encounter in the Sunnah of the Prophet (PBUH), which he laid down for us, that which is from the devil Muslim who commanded him!

Thus, what sort of message is conveyed to the people through these ahadith? Do they confirm the authenticity of the Mohammedan message? Is this the religion that is expected for us to have faith in? Is this how our belief should be regarding the Messenger of Allah (PBUH)? What purpose do these ahadith serve in the propagation of the message of the Prophet (PBUH)? Yet these are the ahadith, and those who memorise them are classified as ulema (scholars)! They shake the minbars of mosques during their sermons with these narrations without being refuted; this pattern is repeated until they become accepted amongst the public to the extent that they constitute a component part of knowledge!

Even if the devil accepted Islam, it is the case that the prerequisite of doing so is the two proclamations of faith;[11] therefore, how can the devil who becomes Muslim and believes in the messenger of Allah (SWT), and who proclaims it as such, have sway over his means of becoming a Muslim by commanding him to do good? Moreover, what type of good? Is the Qur'an part of this good. Is it dictation from the believing devil? We seek the forgiveness of Allah (SWT). There is no strength or power except through Him, the most high!

---

[11]   Shahadatayn: 'There is no god but God. Muhammad is the messenger of God.'

What was the case before the devil became Muslim? In fact, at what time did it accept Islam? This acceptance must have occurred after the introduction of Islam—that is, after its commencement—which would mean that during the beginning of the Prophet's mission, he had a disbelieving devil as a companion! Do these ahadith indicate the honour of the Mohammedan message and the nobility of the one who delivered it? What more would the enemy of Islam want than to paint a picture of a man who is accompanied by the devil and affirm him to be the Messenger of the Muslims? O Allah, we absolve ourselves from this belief, and if not for your forgiveness and mercy, we would indeed be of those who are damned. You are worthy of reverence and adequate for granting forgiveness. O Allah, pray, bless, and send peace, honour, and veneration upon the best of your creation, your beloved, whom you blessed eternally and made a Prophet before the creation of our father Adam. And you have made him a Prophet before blowing soul in him and likewise upon his virtuous family. Through this prayer, forgive all our sins, and increase our love for your beloved, the crown of your perfection, the light of your kingdom, and the focus of your transcendence. Send upon him blessings as befits his nobility, and pray upon him as befits the way you love prayer upon him to be!

11

The Accusation of Circuiting His Wives

It is reported in Sunan Abi Dawud on the authority of Anas that 'the Messenger (PBUH) one night, did circuits with his wives with a single bathing.'[1] This Hadith indicates that the Messenger (PBUH), after fulfilling his need from one of them, headed towards another without bathing. Yet he himself (PBUH) states, 'Cleanliness invites towards faith.'[2] They claim that the Messenger (PBUH) spends the entire night circuiting his wives without having time to pray to his Lord. All the while, Allah (SWT) says, 'Arise the night [to pray], except for a little' (73:2). They tint their tongues with falsehood by depicting him in such a manner and asserting his actions to contradict the command of Allah (SWT). What a heinous attribution!

Allah (SWT) confirms, 'Indeed, your Lord knows, that you stand [in prayer] close to two thirds of the night, and (sometimes) half of it, and (other times) a third of it' (73:20). Who is more truthful in speech than Allah (SWT)? The question remains, how does this Hadith serve the depiction of Islam and invitation to Allah (SWT)? The reality is, it wrongfully lays accusation against the Prophet (PBUH) and is a source of ridicule for those who wish to mock the noble Prophet (PBUH). What is worse, the Hadith is reinforced with another:

---

[1]   Sunan Abi Dawud.
[2]   Jami' As-Saghir Lisuyuti.

Bilal, the ally of Abu Bakr used to raise the Adhan and call the Messenger (PBUH) to come to prayer. One morning he called to the Fajr prayer. It was said to him that the Prophet (PBUH) was sleeping; and so he shouted as loud as he could: "Prayer is better than sleep" Saeed Bin Al-Musayyib stated that due to this incidence, the statement, "Prayer is better than sleep" was added to the Adhan of the Fajr prayer.[3]

It is manifestly apparent that this contradicts the Qur'an. 'Indeed, your Lord knows, that you stand [in prayer] close to two thirds of the night, and (sometimes) half of it, and (other times) a third of it' (73:20). The Prophet (PBUH) also confirmed, 'Oh Aisha, my eyes sleep, but my heart remains awake.'[4] What is more, had Bilal (RA) found the Prophet (PBUH) asleep, sleep would be incumbent upon him in submission to the Messenger (PBUH) since he has no access to the intention of Allah (SWT) regarding what He prescribes through His Messenger (PBUH) to people. There may have been a condition that was introduced regarding the Fajr prayer that Bilal is unaware of.

Above all, comportment with the Messenger (PBUH) is more important than asserting to know the law of Allah (SWT) in his presence or displaying a greater desire than him in fulfilling it! Just as raising one's voice in the presence of the Messenger (PBUH) destroys one's actions, then how would be shouting loudly from behind walls?[5] Furthermore, did the Prophet (PBUH) disobey this command of Allah (SWT): 'Arise the night [to pray], except for a little' (73:2)? Did he sleep instead of pray? Allah (SWT) mentions, 'And when it is said to them, "Come to what Allah has revealed and to the Messenger," they say, "that which we found our fathers upon is enough for us"' (5:104).

Thus, this Hadith serves no purpose in clarifying the manner of delivering the Muhammadan message, rather only to reduce the honour of the one who came with it. Many attempt to use the Hadith

---

3   Musnad Ahmad.
4   Sahih al-Bukhari.
5   See verse 49:4.

to demonstrate the desire of Bilal to establish the prayer as greater than that of the Prophet (PBUH) so as to further prove the point that at times his companions are superior to him, as mentioned previously regarding the captives of Badr.[6]

It is narrated in another Hadith:

> The Prophet (PBUH) awoke [from a dream], and sent for Bilal, questioning him [upon his arrival], 'Oh Bilal, by what means did you manage to enter Paradise before me, for whenever I enter, I hear your footsteps ahead of me? I then approached a lofty, elevated palace of gold and asked: "To whom does this palace belong to?" It was said to me: "A man from amongst the Muslims of the Ummah of Muhammed." I continued: "I'm Muhammed, to whom does this palace belong to?" It was then said: "Umar Bin Al-Khattab."' The Messenger (PBUH) then said: 'Oh Umar, had it not been for your jealousy, I would have entered the palace.' Umar replied: 'Oh Messenger of Allah, how can I feel jealous of you.' Bilal answered: 'Oh Messenger of Allah (SWT), I didn't do anything except that whenever I relieve myself, I make ablution and followed it with two units of prayer.' The Prophet (PBUH) said: 'By this [action you have preceded me in to paradise].'[7]

In other words, due to the number of prayers performed by Bilal, it warranted him entrance into paradise before the Messenger (PBUH)! It is also mentioned that, on occasions, the time of Fajr prayer would arrive and yet the Messenger (PBUH) would be in ritual impurity;[8] he would rise up and commence fasting.[9] This is so that they can attribute to him opposition of this command of Allah: 'Arise the night

---

6   See Chapter 2.
7   Musnad Ahmad.
8   Janabah: ritually impure due to sexual intercourse or seminal discharge.
9   Sahih al-Bukhari.

[to pray], except for a little' (73:2). All the while, Bilal (RA) precedes him into paradise due to his abundant prayers and exertions.

Thus, the Islamic sources state:

- Bilal is more eager to establish the prayer than the Prophet (PBUH).

- Bilal enters paradise before the Prophet.

- The Prophet doesn't know how Bilal entered paradise before him.

- This is qualified with the request of the Prophet (PBUH) seeking to know Bilal's secret of entering paradise first!

- The Prophet (PBUH) remains in conflict with the decree of Allah (SWT) by not standing in the night prayer and instead circuiting his wives with a single bathing!

- When the Fajr prayer sets in, the Prophet (PBUH) is found in ritual impurity or even asleep, and Bilal (RA) has to issue forth an admonition on the top of his voice to urge him to awaken and offer prayers!

This is how many Muslims view the Seal of the Prophets and Messengers, the most noble of creation sent for humans: 'So that he [Muhammad] may bring out those who believe and do good deeds from the recesses of darkness into light' (65:11).

What is also apparent from the above Hadith of al-Bukhari, after confirming that Bilal enters paradise before the Messenger (PBUH), is that it depicts him as one who is astonished by a palace of gold—desiring it—and questions to whom it belongs. Once he was informed that it was Umar's, the Messenger (PBUH) withdrew his desire to enter the palace, fearing the jealousy of Umar! 'There is no strength or might, save Allah's!' The one for whom Allah (SWT) created paradise and bestowed favours upon until he was satisfied is portrayed as one who enters paradise as a total stranger, questioning what it contains, whilst another enters before him, all the while desiring to enter a palace from amongst its palaces! Is this the portrayal of the Prophet and the status of the Messenger (PBUH) amongst the Muslims? 'They have not truly revered Allah, as He truly deserves' (22:74).

12

The Accusation of Praying over a Hypocrite

Allah (SWT) said, 'Say (Oh Muhammad to them): Believe in it or do not believe' (17:107). Thus, He (SWT) established the absence of compulsion[1] for the human being: 'Whoever wishes to believe, believe; and whoever wishes to disbelieve, disbelieve' (18:29). This is nothing but a reminder that one who intends to follow the Messenger (PBUH) should therefore contemplate upon the matter of faith. Indeed, the statement is worthy of full consideration and introspection with an eye intent for the hereafter, a day where neither wealth nor children will be of benefit except the embodied mercy of Allah Almighty, which is His Messenger, the possessor of intercession. Where do we stand in relation to him?

It is not unusual to say that one will not find a Muslim who is unaware of what is said regarding Abdullah bin Salul[2] and his hypocrisy as if it is a pillar among the pillars of Islam to the extent that he has become an icon for setting parables for hypocrisy in the general populace. So what is the significance of maintaining this state of hypocrisy attributed to Abdullah bin Salul? The Prophet (PBUH) said, 'Amongst my companions are twelve hypocrites; eight of them

---

[1] 'Absence of compulsion' is the Qur'anic term equivalent to *freedom*.

[2] A previous king-to-be of Medina during the war of al-Aws and al-Khazraj.

will never enter paradise until a hawser[3] enters through the eye of a needle.[4] This Hadith indicates that being described as a companion of the Prophet does not exclude one from being a hypocrite. And he (PBUH) made the knowledge of who these hypocrites were a secret, unknown to any of his companions except Hudhaifa (RA). None of them were named by him (PBUH), neither Abdullah bin Salul nor anyone else. Despite this, one will find all Muslims today, Sunni and Shiite, confirming the hypocrisy of Abdullah bin Salul.

This matter may appear to be a confirmation of the hypocrisy of Abdullah bin Salul, but analysis attests to the contrary and is far more serious. Indeed, the assertion of hypocrisy upon anyone is not of grave consequence for Islam or Muslims. Therefore, what is the significant issue behind this interest in attesting hypocrisy upon this man?

The answer is that the hidden danger in this situation lies in the fact that it concerns the greatest, most honourable, and noblest of Allah's creation (PBUH) as well as his actions and knowledge; moreover, it is an accusation and declaration of fault against him! Let us then critically examine the subject, so as to discover the truth of what it really indicates, and let us reflect on the following questions:

1. Does anyone have authority to hold the Messenger (PBUH) accountable for his message?

2. Did the Messenger (PBUH) enshroud the corpse of Abdullah bin Salul with his garment and pray upon him?

3. Is not the prayer upon the deceased anything except a supplication for forgiveness?

4. Is it possible for the supplication of the Messenger (PBUH) for forgiveness of another to be unanswered?

5. Does the Messenger (PBUH) not intercede?

---

3   A very thick rope for towing, anchoring, or tying up a ship.
4   Sahih Muslim.

6. Can actions of the Messenger (PBUH) amount to nothing?

7. Did the Messenger (PBUH) disobey his Lord?

8. Can the Messenger (PBUH) be accused of ignorance regarding the Qur'an?

9. Can it be accepted that it is possible to correct the Messenger (PBUH) of his own message?

10. Was there a companion other than Hudhaifa[5] who knew who the hypocrites were?

11. Did the Messenger (PBUH) declare that Abdullah bin Salul was a hypocrite?

12. Did Hudhaifa disclose and spread his secret and proclaim that Abdullah bin Salul is amongst the hypocrites?

13. Was Abdullah bin Salul amongst those who were flogged during the incidence of Ifk,[6] such as Hassan bin Thabit?

14. What of the Hadith that is reported by al-Bukhari, that the one who had the greatest share of responsibility of spreading the slander of Ifk was Hassan bin Thabit?

15. Did Umar bin al-Khattab, during his caliphate, pray the Janazah prayer upon anyone for whom Hudhaifa did not attend?

16. And if neither the Prophet (PBUH) nor Hudhaifa declared the hypocrisy of Abdullah bin Salul, then where did this accusation come from?

---

[5] Known as the possessor of the secret of the Messenger of Allah.
[6] Slander of Ayesha (RA).

Allah (SWT) bestowed knowledge of the hypocrites only upon His Messenger when He said, 'And among the Arabs around you are hypocrites and from the residents of Medina, who have perfected the practice of hypocrisy. You do not know them; We know them' (9:101). Thus, He (SWT) revealed that the Prophet (PBUH) lacked the knowledge of the hypocrites by himself and therefore affirmed for him His own knowledge of them—i.e. He made His knowledge of the hypocrites the knowledge of His Messenger!

The Prophet (PBUH) only informed Hudhaifa (RA) as to who the hypocrites were. Hudhaifa kept this secret without disclosing it despite the attempts of Umar bin al-Khattab, who insisted he reveal them or at least confirm whether he's one of them. Even during his caliphate, he would wait until Hudhaifa attended a funeral prayer, as mentioned in the traditions. So if Hudhaifa prayed, Umar would pray, and if not, then neither would he. This also indicates that the hypocrites should not be prayed upon. So if Hudhaifa didn't pray upon a hypocrite, then it necessarily follows that the one who taught him— the Prophet (PBUH)—would himself never do so since he (PBUH) would never forbid an action and then enact it himself! Moreover, it is inconceivable that he would pray upon one whom Allah (SWT) had forbidden him to pray upon.

Astonishingly, it is reported in Hadith that the Messenger (PBUH), if there was a funeral of a poor person from amongst the Muslims who was unable to repay his debt due to intense poverty and destitution even if it amounted to a single dinar, he would not pray upon this person.[7] Rather, he would say to his companions, 'Pray over your companion.'

It is well known that the Prophet (PBUH) fulfilled the debt of Salman (RA) and of Juwariyyah (RA). He was undeniably the most generous of men to ever walk upon this earth—the mercy of Allah (SWT) for all creation. 'We have not sent you (Oh Muhammad) but as a mercy for all the worlds' (21:107). With him, the poverty-stricken and the destitute were the most happy. He (PBUH) once said, 'Whoever

---

7   Majma' az-Zawaid Lil-Haythami.

honours the wealthy due to his richness, or disdains the poor due to his poverty, will never cease from being damned by Allah (SWT), ever.'[8] Then how is it possible that he would not ensure the debt of the poor and pray over them? Is it the Mohammedan character to pray over a hypocrite and not upon a poor destitute? If it is established that the Prophet did not pray over an indebted, poor person, then the reason is not due to his poverty or debt but rather due a cause that the Prophet (PBUH) was aware of, and that can only be hypocrisy.

It is said that the Prophet (PBUH) did not pray upon the one who passed away if they were poor, destitute, and indebted. And yet he prayed upon the one who is said to be the chief of the hypocrites, Abdullah bin Ubayy bin Salul; enshrouded him with his robe; and stood upon his grave until he was buried.

It is mentioned in Sahih al-Bukhari:

> When Abdullah Bin Ubayy died, his son Abdullah Bin Abdullah came to the Messenger of Allah (PBUH) and requested him for his robe so that he may enshroud his father's body with it. The Prophet gave it to him. He [Abdullah Bin Abdullah] then asked him to pray over him, and so the Messenger of Allah (PBUH) rose up to do so. Subsequently, Umar approached and grasped the robe of the Messenger of Allah (PBUH) and said: 'Oh Messenger of Allah, do you pray over him while Allah Almighty forbade you to do so?' The Messenger of Allah replied: 'Indeed Allah Almighty gave me the option and said: 'Ask forgiveness for them or don't ask for forgiveness for them. If you ask forgiveness for them seventy times—Allah will never forgive them. That is because they disbelieved in Allah and His Messenger, and Allah does not guide the people of immorality,[9] and therefore I will exceed the seventy.' Umar retorted: 'He's a hypocrite.' The Prophet (PBUH) proceeded to pray over him, and consequently

---

8   Lisan ul-Mizan.

9   See the Holy Qur'an verse 9:80.

> Allah revealed: 'And do not pray over any one of them
> who has died—ever—nor stand at his grave.' Indeed, they
> disbelieved in Allah and His Messenger and died while
> they were defiantly sinful. (9:84)

It is clear from the Hadith that Umar objected, based on the verse
'And do not pray over any one of them who has died' when he said
'Do you pray over him while Allah Almighty forbade you to do so?'
The specific verse that prohibits prayer upon the hypocrites is verse 84
from Chapter 9 of Tawbah.[10] Then how can it be said that the Prophet
(PBUH) responded with what he was given the option of doing,
which was to ask forgiveness, and not with what he was forbidden
from doing, which was prayer upon the hypocrites? The option that
was given to the Prophet (PBUH) in verse 80 was to ask forgiveness
for the hypocrites; it does not address praying over them, rather only
of requesting forgiveness. And it precedes the verse of prohibition of
prayer (verse 84). The ground of objection for Umar upon the Prophet
was not asking forgiveness for the hypocrites, rather the prayer!
Then how come the Prophet's (PBUH) response regarded asking for
forgiveness?

We find in this Hadith that the Prophet (PBUH) did not state that
Abdullah bin Salul was indeed a hypocrite, nor did Hudhaifa (RA),
the companion of the Prophet who knew who the hypocrites were.
Neither is it confirmed in any other Hadith that is attributed to the
Prophet (PBUH). In fact, it was Umar who asked Hudhaifa (RA)
who the hypocrites were since he did not know, but Hudhaifa never
disclosed the secret of the Messenger of Allah (PBUH). Indeed, the
person who claimed that Abdullah bin Salul was a hypocrite was Umar
bin al-Khattab, as seen in the Hadith, as well as Aisha in the Hadith
of Ifk![11]

Umar attempted to deter the Messenger (PBUH) from praying upon
Abdullah bin Salul, but the Prophet dismissed Umar's objection when
he grasped him by his robe by drawing it back from him. Thereafter,

---

10   Arabic name of Chapter 9 of the Qur'an, Repentance.
11   Slander that was hurled at Aisha.

Umar stood in front of him, saying is the Messenger going to pray over Abdullah bin Salul when he said such-and-such on such-and-such a day? The Prophet smiled; he then instructed him to step aside so that he could pray over him, to which Umar responded, 'He's a hypocrite.' Nevertheless, the Prophet of Allah (PBUH) prayed upon him. From here it has been concluded that Abdullah bin Salul was a hypocrite, but that is from Umar, who did not know who the hypocrites were! Moreover, it is said he was the chief of the hypocrites, but neither the Prophet (PBUH) nor Hudhaifa (RA) ever claimed such a thing. They were the only two who knew who the hypocrites were.

Thus, hypocrisy was attributed to Abdullah bin Salul by one who had no knowledge of the hypocrites. Insistence upon his hypocrisy continued despite the Prophet (PBUH) enshrouding his body with his robe, praying upon him, and standing at his grave. Why is there such an insistence upon his hypocrisy? Is it to justify Umar's remonstration against the Prophet despite it being inadmissible for him—or for any Muslim—to oppose the Messenger (PBUH) in any action or affair? Indeed, Allah Almighty said, 'Thus, they should not contest with you concerning the matter [of the Message]' (22:67). Or is it to say the position of Umar in his opposition to the Prophet (PBUH) was more correct than the action of the infallible Prophet (PBUH) even though it wasn't based upon knowledge?

It is inconceivable unless it is assumed that he is more knowledgeable than the Prophet concerning the Qur'an and its implementation as well as the fulfilment of the message. Hence, he dares to say to the Messenger of Allah Almighty, upon whom revelation was bestowed, 'Do you pray over him while Allah Almighty forbade you to do so?' as if to admonish him from perpetrating an act that Allah Almighty forbade! What is imperative upon Umar is obedience to the Messenger of Allah, which in fact is obedience to Allah.

Even if Umar in his objection was drawing from the Qur'an on the assumption that the verse of prohibition was revealed before the prayer upon Abdullah bin Salul, which contradicts what the Hadith proposes, he is not more knowledgeable of the Qur'an than the one upon whom it was revealed. He cannot object to the Prophet (PBUH) on grounds of what was revealed of the Qur'an before this as if he is more knowledgeable of it than the Prophet (PBUH)! He is not the clarifier of the Qur'an in the presence of the Prophet (PBUH). Nor is it permitted for him to overstep the Prophet through opposition and seizure of his robe, claiming that he holds the knowledge of the Qur'an and the intention of Allah regarding the message!

I see this as nothing other than harming the Messenger, if what is attributed to Umar is true. If we accept he can do this, it would mean asserting the departure of Umar from obedience to Allah and His Messenger (PBUH). Allah Almighty states, 'Say, "Obey Allah and the Messenger." But if they abstain—then indeed, Allah does not love those who deny the truth' (3:32). Moreover, accepting this would be as if we no longer held such status for the Prophet (PBUH) or faith in him concerning his knowledge of what came from Allah (SWT) in comparison with Umar's knowledge! No Muslim would ever utter this or believe it to be true; we seek refuge from being of those who are ignorant. To uphold such a belief (i.e. that Abdullah bin Salul was in fact a hypocrite) would mean that the prayer of the Prophet, as mentioned, was the target of censure of Allah (SWT) and that Umar was preferred over him!

It is noticeable in the Hadith that Umar states, 'Do you pray over him while Allah Almighty forbade you to do so?' This indicates that the prohibition of prayer upon the hypocrites preceded the prayer of the Prophet over Abdullah bin Salul and his conversation with Umar, as displayed in the Hadith which refutes the claim of Umar (in the same hadith) that the prohibition in the Qur'an was revealed in support of his disagreement. It also confirms that the Prophet (PBUH) prayed over Abdullah bin Salul after the revelation of the verse of prohibition and not before it!

They intended to affirm that Abdullah bin Salul is a hypocrite despite there being no textual evidence from one with such knowledge and then to say that the Prophet (PBUH) prayed upon a hypocrite. Then they said that Umar, who is unaware of the hypocrites, objected against the Messenger of Allah for praying over him as if he was more aware of the hypocrites than the Prophet himself. Furthermore, they alleged that Allah (SWT) advocated Umar by revealing the verse of prohibition in response to his strong dissenting stance against the Messenger in his manner of fulfilling the message over and above the Prophet and for being more aware of who the hypocrites were and the necessary interaction that is afforded to them. Thus, they claim that Allah blamed His Prophet, the city of knowledge, though Allah (SWT) made obedience to his Prophet imperative in the fulfilment of his message (PBUH)!

After establishing in the revealed text that none possesses knowledge of the hypocrites except himself in His statement—'And from the residents of Medina are those who have perfected the practice of hypocrisy. You do not know them; We know them' (9:101)—Allah Almighty informed His Messenger of the hypocrites and commanded him not to pray over them. Thus, having knowledge of the hypocrites is impossible, save for the Messenger of Allah. No one should dare claim having this knowledge except one who informed by the Prophet (PBUH), which was only Hudhaifa (RA)! Being a companion of the Prophet does not negate hypocrisy due to this statement of the Messenger (PBUH): 'Amongst my companions there are twelve hypocrites, from them, eight will never enter paradise until a hawser enters through the eye of a needle.'[12] Thus, there is nothing remaining that surely negates hypocrisy from a companion of the Prophet except prayer of the Prophet upon him or her or the prayer of Hudhaifa after the Prophet (PBUH).

Notice the discrepancy of the Hadith in the statement of Umar when he objected against the Messenger (PBUH): 'Do you pray over him while Allah Almighty forbade you to do so?' This statement indicates that Umar is drawing upon the verse of prohibition: 'And do not pray over any one of them.' Umar says that the Prophet prayed over Abdullah bin Salul, that Allah revealed, 'And do not pray over any one of them'—in other words, Umar objected based upon the verse of prohibition and then claimed that this verse was revealed after his objection!

---

[12] Sahih Muslim.

Notice also that the subject of the Hadith is of prayer upon the hypocrites, as Umar states, 'Do you pray over him while Allah Almighty forbade you to do so?' The response attributed to the Prophet is this: 'Indeed Allah Almighty gave me the option and said: "Ask forgiveness for them or don't ask for forgiveness for them. If you ask forgiveness for them seventy times—Allah will never forgive them. That is because they disbelieved in Allah and His Messenger, and Allah does not guide the people of immorality" (9:80) and therefore I will exceed the seventy.' The divine order is this: 'And do not pray over any one of them.' Hence, it's not a choice in praying over the hypocrites but is rather a choice in the plea for their pardon—yet the subject of the Hadith is prayer. Therefore, invoking for forgiveness has nothing to do with the topic.

The truth of the verse 'And do not pray over any one of them who has died—ever' lies in one of two possibilities. It can either be said that Muhammad, the Messenger of Allah (PBUH), clearly opposed his Lord and prayed upon a hypocrite despite the verse or that Abdullah bin Salul is not from amongst the hypocrites. The accusation that the Prophet contravened divine order is not believable because it would mean that he was not a Messenger, an assertion of disbelievers. 'And those who disbelieve say, "You are not a Messenger"' (13:43).

Therefore, the accusation of Abdullah bin Salul being a hypocrite belittles the actions of the Prophet, ascribing to him fault and, more than that, attributing to him disobedience of his Lord's command and failure in fulfilling the message. It also holds Umar as being more knowledgeable and more capable with the truth and claims that Allah Almighty supported Umar whilst censuring His Prophet for disobeying Umar! In other words, in this scenario, Umar is worthier than the Prophet for prophethood and more acquainted with fulfilling the message and that the Prophet, whom Allah (SWT) chose to fulfil His message, is not suitable or as worthy as Umar! It is as if Allah (SWT) did not make the most appropriate choice for His message!

The greatest share of the spreading of slander during the incidence of Ifk is also attributed to Ibn Salul despite the fact that he was not flogged during this adversity. Nor was the punishment of *qadhf*[13] implemented upon him, as implemented upon Hassan bin Thabit, Mastah, and Hamnah, those who embarked upon its circulation. How can Abdullah bin Salul be the one who had the greater share of this incidence whilst no sufficient evidence was found against him to implement the punishment of qadhf?

The Hadith of Ifk is cited in Sahih al-Bukhari on the authority of Aisha (RA). She said:

> The Messenger of Allah stood up, seeking support for himself against Abdullah Bin Ubayy Bin Salul, and while at the Minbar announced: 'Oh Muslims, who will support me and punish a man, of whom it has reached me, has offended my family; for by Allah I have known nothing from my family except good, and of the man, nothing but good, he has never entered upon my family except with my presence.' Sa'd bin Mu'adh Al-Ansari stood up and said, 'Oh Messenger of Allah, I will deal with him for you. If he is from [the tribe of] Al-Aws,[14] then I will cut off his head, and if he is from our brothers of [the tribe of] Al-Khazraj,[15] order us and we will obey.' Then Sa'd bin Ubadah stood up. He was the leader of Al-Khazraj—the mother of Hassan Bin Thabit was his cousin—and he was before this, a righteous man, but he was overcome by tribal chauvinism[16] and said to Sa'd: 'By Allah, you're a liar, you will not kill him, nor will you ever be able to kill him.' Usayd bin Hudayr, the cousin of Sa'd bin Mu'adh, stood up and answered Sa'd bin Ubadah: 'You're a liar. By Allah, we will kill him. You are a hypocrite, arguing on behalf of the hypocrites!' Both tribes, Al-Aws and Al-Khazraj, became

---

13   *Qadhf*: accusation of unchastity.

14   Al-Aws.

15   Al-Khazraj.

16   This was widespread amongst the Arab tribes before the advent of the Messenger (PBUH).

inflamed until they were about to come to blows, while the
Messenger of Allah was standing at the Minbar.'[17]

Firstly, it is noticeable in this Hadith that it is Aisha (RA) who says
that the Prophet (PBUH) wanted support against Abdullah bin Salul,
not the Prophet himself. Nor does she state that the Prophet says this.
Thus, the Hadith demonstrates that the Prophet does not mention the
accused person by name.

Secondly, the Hadith indicates that the Prophet mentioned these
words before he has ascertained beyond doubt the evidence against the
accused. It is inconceivable that the Prophet would disseminate this
information. Had there been sufficient evidence against Abdullah bin
Salul, then the Prophet (PBUH) would not hesitate to implement the
prescribed punishment upon him, as was implemented upon Hassan
bin Thabit and those with him after the validation of evidence.

Thirdly, why would the Messenger of Allah, the possessor of divine
command, entrust the affair to the community, executing the
punishment of equal retribution against an unnamed defendant after
inciting them against such a person in a public address? How would
the sentence be carried out? What is the sentence? Is it flogging, the
death penalty, or some other punishment?

Fourthly, note the statement of Sa'd bin Mu'adh, the chief of al-Aws:
'If he is from [the tribe of] al-Aws, then I will cut off his head.' This is
despite the fact that the crime, if confirmed and the accused known,
its punitive measure is flogging and not beheading since it was *qadhf*!

Furthermore, Aisha makes mention of the mother of Hassan bin
Thabit, the cousin of Sa'd bin Ubadah, the leader of al-Khazraj, who
was overcome by tribal chauvinism and clashed with Sa'd bin Mu'adh!
This implies—if the Hadith is true—that the Prophet sought the
punishment of Hassan bin Thabit and not Abdullah bin Salul since it
was Hassan who was flogged in the incidence of Ifk!

---

[17]   Sahih al-Bukhari.

Again, notice in the statement of Aisha (RA) that Sa'd bin Ubadah was a righteous man but was overcome by tribal chauvinism and responded to Sa'd bin Mu'adh with 'By Allah, you're a liar, you will not kill him, nor will you ever be able to kill him.' This suggests that the tribal chauvinism was specifically for the sake of Hassan bin Thabit. Sa'd bin Mu'adh did not say that he would kill him if he was from al-Khazraj, rather he said to the Messenger of Allah (PBUH): 'If he is from our brothers of [the tribe of] Al-Khazraj, order us and we will obey.'

Look at the inevitable consequences of such a sermon that is attributed to the Prophet (PBUH): death for the crime of qadhf. And the implementation of the ruling is being left for the masses, not for the judge or the ruler, and without substantiation of evidence against the accused, who is unknown at this point! Is it conceivable to accept that the Prophet (PBUH) was powerless to investigate the claims and ascertain the truth or to implement the sharia[18] ruling upon the accused, whoever that person happened to be?

Fifthly, the statement of Sa'd bin Mu'adh clarifies that it is not known from which tribe the accused is, al-Aws or al-Khazraj, or what his name is since the Prophet (PBUH) did not mention Abdullah ibn Salul or anyone else by name.

Sixthly, the implementation of the hadd[19] punishment upon Hassan bin Thabit, Mastah, and Hamnah, indicates that there was an investigation, a hearing of evidence, and a carrying out of the ruling, which did not include Abdullah bin Salul. Thus, how can credence be given to this Hadith and this sermon that is attributed to the Messenger of Allah (PBUH), wherein the accused and the ruling are unidentified?

Furthermore, notice the painting of the companions that is portrayed and their interaction with the Prophet, their accusation of one another of hypocrisy, and the weakness of their relationship between one

---

18   Legal legislation.
19   Prescribed.

another. Is this how the Prophet and his companions are imagined? Anyone who wishes to accept all that is contained in Sahih al-Bukhari, let them reflect on their position before laying blame at the one who refuses to accept all that it contains.

Another Hadith found in Sahih al-Bukhari mentions:

> Masruq said: 'I entered upon Aisha (RA) while Hassan bin Thabit was with her reciting to her from some of his poetic verses . . . I said to her, "Why do you grant him admittance, though Allah said: '. . . and as for him among them, who had the greater share therein, his will be a severe torment'" (24:11). She replied, "And what punishment is greater than blindness?"'[20]

It is indicative from this Hadith that it was Hassan who had the 'greater share' of the incidence of Ifk and not Ibn Salul. Who was it then that claimed that Ibn Salul was a hypocrite or that he was the chief of the hypocrites? The Prophet (PBUH) never affirmed this since he would not divulge that which he meant to be kept secret; neither did Hudhaifa, the possessor of such a secret. And none other than them knew who the hypocrites were!

If we were to presume that the prohibition of prayer upon the hypocrites came after the Prophet (PBUH) had prayed upon Ibn Salul and that he was indeed a hypocrite, as it is claimed, does this invalidate the prayer that the Prophet had prayed, revoking its blessing from the person prayed upon or prohibiting similar actions in the future? Is what is intended for Muslims, as is occurring at present, that they see the prayer of the Prophet upon Ibn Salul and his enshrouding him with his robe as something without worth, that what the Prophet did was out of ignorance and was futile, or that he disobeyed his Lord? Yet we continue to curse the one upon whom the Prophet (PBUH) himself prayed and for whose forgiveness the Prophet supplicated in prayer! Furthermore, there are those who consider that the Prophet (PBUH) prayed for his forgiveness openly whilst supplicating against

---

[20]   Sahih al-Bukhari.

him in secret! This type of character is not attributable to the lowest of the Muslims who is truthful with Allah Almighty and has sincerity in speech and action, let alone being attributable to the Prophet (PBUH), who was sent to perfect moral character. What would be the response of the believer if he is questioned that if the Prophet indeed prayed upon Ibn Salul and invoked for his forgiveness, then would he do that upon the footsteps of the Prophet? Would the believer pray, following the Prophet (PBUH), or refrain and thus affirm his accusation of the Messenger (PBUH)?

In fact, there is nothing that can compel the Prophet (PBUH) to perform a matter in religion that neither he nor Allah—who sent him with the truth and made him the best example to follow for truthfulness, sincerity, and strength in clarity of the truth without compromise—wants. To demonstrate this resoluteness, the Prophet (PBUH) did not hesitate to forbid Umar himself from leading the Muslims in prayer when he heard him leading Maghrib[21] by saying, 'Allah (SWT) will never accept this, nor the Muslims.'[22] No Muslim would believe that in Umar there is more resolve for the truth than the Prophet unless Umar is his Messenger!

Whoever believes that Umar is more unwavering than the Prophet in exposing and establishing the truth has indeed degraded himself by lowering his perception of the status of the Messenger (PBUH), who is the best example to be followed, and made the status of Umar superior, adopting him as his best example of the truth!

Whoever diminishes the exalted Muhammadan status is not a Muslim! Those who hold to this corrupt belief view the forthcoming Esa (AS)[23] as being in opposition to Ahlu Sunnah.[24] They are the majority who will fight him and oppose his way of reviving the Sunnah, manifesting true faith and clarifying the exalted status of the Prophet (PBUH), who is peerless whether compared to Umar (RA) or

---

[21] Evening prayer.
[22] Abu Dawud.
[23] Return of Jesus (AS).
[24] Those who uphold the way of the Prophet (PBUH).

anyone else. Indeed, Allah (SWT) shall clarify through him (Esa) the vision of those whose eyes were blinded from seeing the condemnation of the umma for the Prophet for over fourteen hundred years.

Perhaps their intention in absolving Umar from fault and elevating his status is to exonerate the companion of the Messenger of Allah from disobedience to Allah Almighty. Since it would otherwise exclude him from companionship and, moreover, from being obedient to Allah (SWT), as obedience to the Prophet is obedience to Allah Almighty. 'Whoever obeys the Messenger has indeed obeyed Allah, and we have not sent you as a guardian over them!' (4:80). 'Say, "Obey Allah and the Messenger." But if they turn away then indeed, Allah does not love the disbelievers' (3:32). How can the second caliph be stigmatised with disobedience to Allah (SWT) and His Messenger during the life of the Prophet whilst it's out of the question for them to reject a Hadith of Sahih al-Bukhari! Due to this preservation of everything found in al-Bukhari, the Hadith that depicts Umar as disobedient is accepted, and then they justify this disobedience!

This is why they hold on to the position that all the actions of the second caliph are righteous and sound, as mentioned in al-Bukhari, even if they would be in opposition to the Prophet (PBUH)! In order to avoid the risk of stigmatising Umar with disobedience to Allah, they say that the Qur'an came endorsing his position so that his disobedience to the Messenger of Allah should not be disobedience to Allah (SWT). 'They want to segregate between Allah and His Messengers' (4:150). They separate obedience to the Messenger of Allah from obedience to Allah! In fact, they claim that obedience to Allah is possible whilst disobeying the Messenger of Allah and that obedience to Allah (PBUH) is not conditional to the obedience to the Messenger of Allah despite this affirmation by Allah (SWT): 'They say: "We believe in some and deny others."' We obey Allah but not His Messenger: 'Wanting to create a dividing path between them' (4:150).

All this is due to the fear that in Islam, especially amongst the contemporaries of the Prophet (PBUH), there may be companions who commit mistakes! They wish to portray an angelic picture and infallibility of the first Muslims, as mentioned in al-Bukhari, even if it distorts the basis of the truth and asserts mistakes by the Messenger of Allah (PBUH). They wish to depict the great personalities of Islam, specifically the companions of the Prophet, as infallible, as specified in al-Bukhari. Even if one of them disobeys the Prophet himself, he would still be upon the truth, whilst the Prophet would be in error. Moreover, they are, according to this, all free from hypocrisy, and all of them are upright and reliable despite the fact that the Prophet (PBUH) said in Sahih Muslim, 'Amongst my companions there are twelve hypocrites, of whom eight will never enter paradise until a hawser enters through the eye of a needle.'[25]

Allah Almighty says, 'Oh believers [people of Muhammad], do not be like those who abused Moses; then Allah cleared him from what they said. And to Allah he was one distinguished' (33:69). They were in fact the disbelievers from amongst the Jews. Allah says, 'Oh believers [people of Muhammad], do not raise your voices above that of the Prophet or address him loudly in speech like the loudness amongst yourselves, lest your deeds become nullified, while you are unaware' (49:2). And He said, 'Oh you who have come to believe, when you converse privately, do not converse about sin and aggression and disobedience to the Messenger' (58:9). All this is for those who were unaware of the status of the Prophet and his nobility until Allah Almighty rebuked them for bad etiquette and for raising their voices above his to the extent that He forbade them to speak to the Prophet with a raised voice, as practised amongst themselves.

How many of them left the Messenger (PBUH) standing at the sanctuary and absented his mosque for the purposes of entertainment (like listening to a singing maid) or for competing with each other for the purchasing of goods that arrived from Syria? 'Yet [it does happen that] when they become aware of [an occasion for] worldly gain or a passing delight, they rush headlong towards it, and leave you standing' (62:11).

Despite the Qur'an being revealed in their presence and knowing that the wives of the Prophet are their mothers, one will find amongst

---

25   Sahih Muslim.

the companions who used to enter the houses of the Prophet one displaying a level of decadence and misconduct and coveting the wives of the Prophet (PBUH)! This has been confirmed by Allah Almighty in His revelation. Ibn Salul was not of those who entered the houses of the Prophet. Allah Almighty said, 'Oh wives of the Prophet, you are not like any other women. If you truly fear Allah, then do not be soft in speech (to men), lest he in whose heart is disease should covet' (33:32). Therefore, Allah Almighty forbade entering the dwellings of the Prophet without prior permission since there were those who coveted the wives of the Prophet (PBUH) and that used to hurt the Prophet!

One will find from amongst them who is eager for harm to befall the Prophet (PBUH) in a way not expected even from an ordinary Muslim. Whilst (it is claimed) he is guaranteed paradise, he says, 'If Muhammad dies, I will definitely marry Aisha.'[26] And in another narration, he says, 'Why does Muhammad refrain us from our cousins, and yet marry our women? If he dies, we shall marry his wives after him.'[27] What's more, it is claimed that this person is amongst those guaranteed paradise—presuming it to be true—and says 'Muhammad' without an expression of respect or invoking prayers upon him and thereupon anticipating his death so as to marry his wives after him! There is an attempt to exonerate this companion from this repugnant position that no Muslim or disbeliever would dare to take and thus make him one of those guaranteed paradise! They do so without taking heed of the statement of Allah (SWT), nor do they consider the consequent harm directed at the Messenger (PBUH).

Can it be assumed that because he was wishing for the death of the Prophet and impatiently waiting to marry his wives after him, paradise was guaranteed for him? Is it because of this repugnant statement—a statement that is not possible to be attributed to the vagabonds or fools of Medina, a statement harmful to the Prophet (PBUH) and his entire umma—that he is guaranteed paradise? Despite the revelation

---

[26] This statement is attributed Talha ibn Ubaydullah in Al-Hawi Lil-Fatawi.

[27] Ibn Abi Hatim.

of Allah (SWT) regarding him, 'It is not permitted for you to harm the Messenger of Allah or to marry his wives after him, ever. Indeed, that is an enormity in the sight of Allah' (33:52), they made him amongst those who were guaranteed paradise! There is nothing left for those who believe this but to say to the one who harms the Messenger (PBUH): 'Congratulations, oh one who is guaranteed paradise!' Likewise, they say that Allah (SWT) may send down revelation supporting the positions of the one who is in opposition to the Prophet and criticise his Prophet, the city of knowledge, the greatest of creation from amongst His prophets and angels, and upon whom He, the Living, the Everlasting, showers blessings!

13

The Accusation That the Messenger (PBUH) Is Unnecessary for One's Connection to Allah (SWT)

Allah (SWT) says: 'And when My servants ask you (Oh Muhammad) about Me, then I am near; responding to the supplication of the supplicator when he calls. So let them respond to Me, and believe in Me, so that they may be guided' (2:186).

This verse in fact inherently displays praise of the Prophet (PBUH) and indicates the eminence of his knowledge of Allah (SWT), which surpasses all creation, and thus he became the guide for those who ask about Him (SWT). However, those who are unable to fathom the greatness of this verse because of their dense perception, narrow-minded intellect, and shrouded hearts understood from it that the Messenger of Allah (SWT) is unnecessary in connecting with Allah! Had they reflected with the eye of foresight and not of haste, of contemplation rather than neglect, they would find themselves in need of the Messenger (PBUH) even for their compilations of geography, physics, and mathematics, not to mention language itself! How can they deem the Prophet (PBUH), the supreme teacher, as dispensable in regard to the weightiest book that excludes nothing of existence, neither of knowledge nor creation?

This teacher embarked on the interpretation of this book from the words of Allah (SWT), who spoke without organ, language, or voice intelligible to the human being, into the language of Arabic with a clear Arabic tongue. Allah (SWT) extols, 'Indeed, this [Qur'an] is the word of an exalted Messenger' (69:40). How can one dispense with this teacher, who explained this book of Allah (SWT) and all that it contains, and claim that he—the one who encompassed the all-encompassing book and articulated it in the Arabic tongue—is unnecessary? By what rationality can there be no urgent need for the teacher of the highest knowledge, the knowledge of Allah (SWT) that all the messengers came with?

In reality, this is the essential teaching that all the chosen messengers conveyed: 'We never sent a Messenger before you without revealing to him: "There is no god but Me. So worship only Me"' (21:25). The messengers represent the complete words of Allah (SWT), and the greatest in rank amongst them is the Messenger (PBUH), the master of the children of Adam (AS). From them, the covenant of faith in the Messenger (PBUH) and support of him was undertaken. 'Behold that which I have given you of the Scripture and wisdom and then there comes to you a Messenger confirming what is with you, you have to believe in him and support him' (3:81). The Messenger (PBUH) said, 'I was sent as a teacher.' And what is knowledge except that of words? And amongst them are the perfect words.[1] The one who clings to them is protected from the devil, from the gazes of the two beings,[2] and from misguidance. Thus, he started his spiritual journey covertly and openly, adhering to the path of the one who was sent by Allah (SWT) for his guidance and all creation—our master, intercessor, and beloved, Prophet Muhammad (PBUH), whom Allah (SWT) made his love, true faith. Obedience to Allah and our taking of His message are only through the Messenger (PBUH). Those who believe that taking of the message should be directly from Allah (SWT) are the ones who say

---

[1]   Referring to the supplication of the Prophet (PBUH): 'I seek refuge in the perfect words of Allah, from every devil and harmful creature, and from every evil eye' (Bukhari).

[2]   Humanity and jinn.

that Allah (SWT) is not in need of one to guide them to Him. Indeed they are arrogant, ignorant, and misguided.

The reality is that Allah (SWT) is in need of none since He is independent of all existence. But He elects whomever He wills for whatsoever He wills, and He is not questioned regarding His doing. Allah (SWT) is neither impotent in delivering the revelation to each person in his abode, nor is He impotent without the presence of Gabriel (AS) between himself and His noble Messenger, even though the Messenger (PBUH) is closer to Allah (SWT) than Gabriel (AS) since the station of Gabriel (AS) is that of the lote tree,[3] whilst the station of the Messenger is *nearer* to Allah (SWT) than being *face-to-face*. The word *or* mentioned in the verse 'Until he was face-to-face [with Him], or nearer' (53:9) is not one of doubt. Far is Allah (SWT) above having doubt in His speech! Neither is Allah (SWT) incapable of doing away with Messengers and allowing for a direct relationship between the human being and himself, as deemed to be the case by those with twisted understandings and obscured intellects. 'There is not within their hearts except pride, that they are unable to reach' (49:56).

Allah (SWT), in the verse 'And when My servants ask you (Oh Muhammad) about Me, then I am near; responding to the supplication of the supplicator when he calls' (2:182), directs His servants to His Messenger if they seek to arrive at gnosis of Him so that He (SWT) may answer them and answer His Messenger. This path of gnosis and means of interaction with Allah (SWT) is unattainable except through the pathway of the one whom He sent, made beloved, and praised. What is understood from the verse by those with obscured intellect is this: 'And when My servants ask Me, then I am near, responding to the supplication of the supplicator when he calls.' They are unaware or rather unable to see with the eye of deliberation. 'Do they not reflect upon the Qur'an, or are their hearts locked?' (47:24).

---

[3] The furthest boundary (see verse 53:16).

In fact, the speech of Allah (SWT) regarding the verse is addressed to the Prophet (PBUH). It is not addressed to them directly! This is so that the Messenger (PBUH) clarifies for those who ask him with the manners of a student, whilst realising his status, in what manner one interacts with Allah (SWT). Hence, Allah (SWT) says, 'And when My servants ask you (Oh Muhammad) about Me,' conditioning the response upon asking the Messenger (PBUH). None can reach Allah (SWT) or attain gnosis without the Messenger. It is he who acquainted them with Allah (SWT) and thus the condition of this verse is fulfilled: 'Then I am near; responding to the supplication of the supplicator when he calls.' Thus the authorised referrer to Allah (SWT) is the Messenger (PBUH), who teaches His servants closeness to Him, since He (SWT) does not accept the supplication of a heart that is heedless or one whose livelihood is from forbidden sources. Neither is the supplication of one accepted except through the path of the Messenger since he is the teacher and the *city of knowledge*, as he (PBUH) described himself.

This truth is manifested on account of those who wrong themselves and seek respite in Allah (SWT) and the expiation of their foul deeds. Whoever arrives at the door of Allah (SWT) by way of His beloved and Messenger will find Allah (SWT) all forgiving and all merciful: 'And if, when they wrong themselves, come to you (Oh Muhammad) and ask forgiveness of Allah and the Messenger asks forgiveness for them, they would find Allah All-Forgiving and All-Merciful' (4:64). Likewise those whose insight is obscured, understand from this verse: 'And if, when they wrong themselves, ask forgiveness of Allah.' They are unable to fathom the words 'come to you', which determines the theme of the verse. Hence, whoever travels to Medina and asks for forgiveness at the location of the Prophet's burial chamber[4] (even if this is after his departure to his Lord), his situation is unlike the one who visits the Kaaba and asks for forgiveness there. This is notwithstanding the fact that a good deed in Makkah amounts to a hundred thousand fold; nevertheless, finding Allah (SWT) *all forgiving and all merciful* is conditioned upon reaching the Messenger (PBUH) in Medina and not to the Kaaba!

---

4   That is present at Masjid an-Nabawi in al-Madina al-Munwarah.

Allah (SWT) says, 'And if, when they wrong themselves, come to you (Oh Muhammad) and ask forgiveness of Allah and the Messenger asks forgiveness for them, they would find Allah All-Forgiving and All-Merciful' (4:64). The consequence of the verse remains until the end of time and is not null and void after the departure of the Messenger (PBUH) to the Supreme Companion. If this was the case, then the verse would have been similar to the stories that are related from the past, containing how the companions interacted with him, just as the nations of old.

Allah (SWT) says, 'So let them respond to Me.' But did the servants respond to Him (SWT)? How can they know they responded to Allah (SWT) if the Messenger doesn't confirm it since he (PBUH) 'believes in Allah and believes for the believers' (9:61)? Moreover, the Messenger, being kind and merciful to the believers, is concerned over them and thus sends prayers upon them since his prayers are a solace for them. 'And send prayers upon them (O Muhammad). Indeed, your prayer is a solace for them' (9:103). Allah (SWT) says regarding the most beloved to Him of all His creation, 'He is concerned over you and to the believers he is kind and merciful' (9:128). However, did the servants respond to Allah (SWT)? Indeed, the response to Allah (SWT) is responding to His Messenger, as mentioned by Him, 'Respond to Allah and to the Messenger when he calls you to that which revitalises you'⁵ (8:24).

How can the one who is cut off due to arrogance consider that, in achieving closeness to Allah (SWT), he is not in need of the Prophet, the teacher (PBUH)? This is nothing other than self-inequity. And this is despite the fact that Allah (SWT) clarifies that if one is to ask for forgiveness in the presence of the beloved Messenger, one will find Allah (SWT) all forgiving and all merciful. Does not this divine

---

5   Human life has three levels. The first is the animal life, which starts in the womb for 120 days. The second level is when the angel blows the *ruh*, or spirit into the foetus, and thus becomes a person. And then when the person responds to the call of Allah and his Messenger and accepts the revelation, the real life is achieved because the revelation (which revitalises) is ruh, or spirit, as in 42:52.

consignment display the distinction of the Messenger in the sight of Allah (SWT)? He made performing worship of Him in the presence of the Messenger conditional to accepting it, unlike performing it in another place, be it the holy house of Allah in Makkah? Then why the disdain in taking the Messenger (PBUH) as the teacher and criterion and the claim that one is not in need of him in reaching Allah (SWT)?

It is narrated in a Hadith that the Prophet (PBUH) called for one of his companions who happened to be praying and therefore did not respond until he had concluded. The Prophet (PBUH) questioned him regarding the cause of delay, at which point, the companion replied, 'I was praying oh Messenger of Allah.' To this, the Prophet (PBUH) said, 'Did you not hear the statement of Allah (SWT): ". . . respond to Allah and to the Messenger when he calls you to that which revitalises you"?'[6] This is because obedience to the Messenger is obedience to Allah (SWT), without distinction! Whosoever does not uphold obedience to the Messenger at this status and reality has in fact contravened Allah (SWT) since He did not distinguish between obedience to Him and that to Prophet Muhammad (PBUH); therefore, beware of deviating from this intent, 'And they seek to discriminate between Allah and His Messengers', by their claim, 'And they seek to adopt a way in between' (4:150).

Hence, under no circumstances can one be obedient to Allah (SWT) whilst being at conflict with the Messenger (PBUH), just as one who refuses to shorten his prayer whilst travelling, believing it to be Sunnah whilst contravening the Sunnah of the Prophet (PBUH); this is lack of obedience to him (PBUH), which is contravening Allah (SWT). This is sin, not worship. There can be no Sunnah in opposition to the Sunnah of the Prophet (PBUH)! No justification, for not shortening the prayer, can be drawn from the status of the one who established it[7] since he initiated a matter that contradicts what was practised by the Prophet (PBUH), obedience to whom is obedience to Allah; and its burden, as well as the burden of all those who follow it, shall be

---

6   Sunan Abu Dawod.
7   Uthman bin Affan, the third caliph.

upon the establisher. All those who contravene the Messenger have disobeyed him and, as a consequence, have disobeyed Allah (SWT). 'He who obeys the Messenger has indeed obeyed Allah' (4:80).

Allah (SWT) says, 'And believe in Me.' Faith in Allah (SWT) is conditional upon having faith in His book and Messenger. 'O you who believe, be conscious of Allah and believe in His Messenger' (57:28). He has commanded 'those who have faith' in His book to adhere to the Prophet (PBUH), as he is the ultimate authority[8] and thus nothing should be taken except from him and from all his forbiddances they should refrain. He has confided all the matter of the message to the Messenger, saying, 'And whatever the Messenger consigns unto you, take it, and from whatever he forbids you, abstain' (59:7), and He (SWT) warned those who contravene him, 'Let those who contravene the Prophet's order beware' (24:63). Allah designated that obedience to the Messenger is obedience to Him (SWT), without distinction. 'Whoever obeys the Messenger has indeed obeyed Allah' (4:80). Thus, whoever contravenes the Messenger (PBUH) has fallen out of obedience with Allah (SWT).

No one should claim that he can be in obedience to Allah (SWT) whilst being disobedient to the Messenger (PBUH) since this would mean that to him the Prophet (PBUH) has contravened Allah (SWT) and his disobedience to the Prophet is obedience to Allah! This position eliminates one's faith in the Messenger of Allah and his obedience; likewise, it eliminates faith in his message, negating the divine regulations, precepts of ultimate authority, and gnosis of Allah (SWT). Allah (SWT) clarifies that obedience to the Messenger (PBUH) is obedience to Him, but this position claims that disobedience to the Messenger (PBUH) can implicate obedience to Allah (SWT), as forwarded by the ahadith of the captives of Badr, where they said that objection to the Prophet (PBUH) was obedience to Allah.

There is no might or power save with Allah! It has been asserted that opposition to the Messenger's prayer upon Abdullah ibn Salul was

---

8   Marjiyyah al-Ulyaa.

also obedience to Allah (SWT) for the notion that the Messenger (PBUH) is in violation of Allah (SWT)! This assumption is quite impossible since obedience to the Prophet (PBUH) will never part from the obedience to Allah (SWT). Who has the authority to claim that obedience to the Messenger on occasions can be disobedience to Allah (SWT)? Who has the audacity, let alone the superiority, to allege that on occasions the Messenger (PBUH) contravened his Lord and therefore obedience on such occasions are not mandatory and thereafter propose an alternative? And who are the followers of such a person in this belief that inform us that indeed Allah (SWT) has transferred the necessity of following the Messenger (PBUH) to this superior individual on such an occasion by means of abrogation[9] of the verse 'Whoever obeys the Messenger has indeed obeyed Allah' (4:80)? Or who has claimed and implied that the abrogation of its ruling, so as to make contravening the Messenger acceptable, is obedience to Allah (SWT)? What is more is their admiration of such a person who has claimed that Allah (SWT) on such occasions supported him and abandoned His Messenger (PBUH) and reproached him for not accepting the conflicting view of his opponent! O Allah (SWT), we absolve ourselves from such beliefs, and may Your prayers be upon Your Messenger and his virtuous family. Indeed, the Prophet (PBUH) mentioned, 'No Messenger has been disparaged as I have been disparaged.'

Performing actions for the sake of reward is the practice of majority of the umma, believing that entry to paradise is due to actions and not by the mercy of Allah (SWT). An employee will not be entitled to remuneration unless he performs his duty with competence and integrity. It is from the teachings of the Messenger (PBUH), who said, 'Indeed, Allah (SWT) loves, if one is to perform an action, to perform it with competence.' Thus, the sense of satisfaction for the seekers of reward is when they are given the reward because it is the sign of the pleasure of Allah (SWT) and the indication of success for the person. However, if the remunerator is fully discerning, then the threshold for reward (i.e. competency) is difficult to achieve, hence the saying 'He who is taken to account is damned' and likewise the Hadith 'The

---

[9]   Naskh.

wise, is the one who criticises himself[10] and strives for what is after death.'[11]

The reality of actions (collective actions such as buying and selling, carpentry or construction)—there is recompense or reward for them in the hereafter since they shape the scales of the Muslim whether the actions were good or bad. However, if the performer of the actions possesses good character, then this is the heaviest of actions upon the scales on the Day of Judgement. Thereafter, whoever is given his reward is successful and has achieved happiness. Allah (SWT) says, 'Indeed you will be given your full reward on the Day of Judgement.' And after the fulfilment of reward, which is determined by the scales, none shall enter paradise except by mercy. 'Whereupon he that shall be drawn away from the Fire and admitted to Paradise has attained success' (3:185).

Success is admittance to paradise. Allah (SWT) has made the Messenger (PBUH) a support and facilitator to such an end— particularly for those whose scales are stirring with major sins. The Prophet (PBUH) testified, 'My intercession is for the major sinners of my Ummah.'[12] So rest your hopes, O you who love the Prophet (PBUH), upon him since he is the rescuer and deliverer for the one to whom fire is apt recompense! Don't rest your hopes upon your actions, as it opens the path to them being rejected due to the possibility of mistakes, insincerity, and deficiency found within them. Indeed, Allah (SWT) may not even open the door of acceptance for them in the first place!

Consider your actions, in your eyes, as major sins so that the beloved (PBUH) will intercede for you. Perform your deeds upon the footsteps of the beloved (PBUH) in obedience to him, not for the sake of reward, so that you may avoid divine account. Indeed, the seeker of reward is taken to account for his actions, and whoever is taken to account is damned. Having recourse to the Messenger (PBUH) secures

---

[10]　For failure.

[11]　Musnad Ahmad.

[12]　Musnad Ahmed.

the forgiveness of Allah (SWT) upon His servants. Allah (SWT) says, 'And if, when they wrong themselves, come to you (Oh Muhammad) and ask forgiveness of Allah and the Messenger asks forgiveness for them, they would find Allah All-Forgiving and All-Merciful' (4:64). The consequence of the verse remains, and the promise of Allah (SWT) is true.

And who is more true to his word than He (SWT)? Nor did He (SWT) break His promise after the departure of the Prophet (PBUH), and thus the condition in this verse holds true until the Day of Judgement. 'And if when . . . they come to you.' Thus, whoever travels to Medina and asks forgiveness of Allah (SWT) at the noble burial chamber, indeed the Messenger (PBUH) will also ask forgiveness for him, and thus he fulfils the condition.

The remembrance of Allah (SWT) is necessary at all times and places and in every condition. This remembrance necessitates sincerity towards Allah (SWT) and must be void of hypocrisy, the hidden shirk,[13] and self-adulation, regarding which the Prophet (PBUH) said, 'Had you not sinned, I would fear for you that which is greater than sin, self-adulation.' In addition, it necessitates absence of self-conceit, which is the obstinacy of the soul towards pride, regarding which the Prophet (PBUH) said, 'None who has pride shall enter paradise.'[14] And finally, there's the need to conclude the remembrance with proficiency since the Hadith says, 'Indeed, Allah (SWT) loves, if one is to act, to perfect it.'

Prior to all these preconditions, however, an honest intention is essential, as mentioned in the Hadith: 'The intention of a person is better than their action.' Thereafter, the action is submitted to Allah (SWT)—the all-discerning majesty, possessor of glory, the omnipotent—if indeed the action is worthy to be presented to Him in the first place. In reality, it is due to His might and power that our actions are undertaken. But has one rendered thanks to Him? Is it not possible that Allah (SWT) designated us as being from the

---

13 Polytheism.
14 Ibn Majah.

people of sin? If He (SWT) is to reject an action, then this is absolute justice since strength or ability is primarily from Allah (SWT). The performed action, if executed proficiently, is between acceptance and rejection. Thus, the one who clings to his actions and depends upon them to deliver him salvation places his soul in a precarious position of uncertainty since it may not be accepted by the one who 'is not questioned about what He does' (21:23) and such a rejection is destined for an abyss of fire. The actions of Allah (SWT) are all justice since there is no strength or ability except through Him. And so from where shall salvation come?

It is critical that one acts proficiently and with sincerity to God, seeking no reward since 'he who is taken to account is damned'! Let it be that one places his deeds, even those that were proficient and sincere, on the side of one's misdeeds, rather amongst the major sins, and then be certain of salvation! It is the major sinners who will surrender their affair to one whose intercession is guaranteed, and thus the Messenger (PBUH) will safeguard them from the fire. They despair that their actions will avail them, and they abandon self-dependence, considering themselves amongst the damned, and thereupon take recourse with the beloved (PBUH), who guaranteed, 'My intercessions are for the major sinners of my Ummah.'[15] It is they who 'come to you (Oh Muhammad) and ask forgiveness of Allah' for their deeds, be they sound or unsound. The one who deems his deeds sound should likewise ask forgiveness for attributing them to himself, as the strength or ability is not his; in fact, he is empty-handed and void of actions!

Thus, to whom shall one have recourse? The pretenders to Tawhid declare, 'To Allah (SWT).' However, if one wants to find Allah (SWT) all forgiving and all merciful, recourse should be to the one whom Allah (SWT) Himself wants his creation to have recourse to. If one is to have recourse to Allah (SWT) alone, without His beloved, he will find Him almighty, impartial, severe in punishment. Allah (SWT) wills it that one requests His forgiveness and pardon by means of going to the Messenger (PBUH) and requesting forgiveness of Allah

---

[15]   Musnad Ahmed.

(SWT) in his presence, not in the presence of His holy house, and requesting that the Messenger seek forgiveness for them. Following this trajectory and treading upon this path, Allah (SWT) has guaranteed that they will find Him as they had hoped, all forgiving and all merciful. 'And the Messenger asks forgiveness for them, they would find Allah All-Forgiving and All- Merciful' (4:64). And if one is not given the opportunity to visit Medina, then a request should be made to one who is able to request forgiveness on one's behalf. Indeed, the brothers of Yusuf (AS) appealed, 'Oh our father, ask forgiveness of our sins for us' (12:97).

The major sinners have been guaranteed intercession by this statement of the Messenger (PBUH): 'My intercession is for the major sinners of my Ummah.'[16] What is better than performing one's obligations with proficiency and thereafter considering oneself amongst the major sinners, coupled with constant prayer upon the guaranteed intercessor, with whom salvation is attained on the day when the Messengers proclaim, 'Myself, myself'? The one who encounters Allah (SWT) with the Prophet (PBUH), having full dependence upon him whilst despairing of one's actions and being certain of his intercession, will be enveloped in the shade of his vast dignity and receive guaranteed salvation through him. He who considers himself amongst the monotheists, in no need of the Messenger (PBUH) or his intercession, or rather doubts the intercession itself and wishes to meet Allah (SWT) with his actions, Allah (SWT) is in no need of his actions, nor do his actions increase anything in the kingdom of God! Indeed, such a person exposes himself to reckoning before the critical, all-discerning, and all-aware Allah (SWT), who is not questioned regarding His doing.

What a harsh reckoning on the Day of Reckoning! On that day, humanity will be presented before the Lord of the worlds. 'And what one has done of evil, will wish that between it and oneself a long span of time' (3:30). Thereafter, what to say of what follows the reckoning? Paradise will be entered by none save through the mercy of Allah (SWT). He who is not overtaken by His mercy after reckoning will

---

[16]   Musnad Ahmed.

not be delivered even if his actions rival the angels'! Thus, the one who depends upon his actions without hope for the mercy of Allah (SWT) is damned. He who recognises mercy should cling to it since it will be the cause of entry to paradise. And what is the mercy of Allah (SWT) other than the Messenger of Allah (PBUH)? 'And We have not sent you (Oh Muhammad) but as mercy for all the worlds' (21:107). The Messenger (PBUH) said, 'Oh people, indeed I am a gift of mercy.'[17]

O Allah, send prayers upon our master, Muhammad, your Messenger, the gift of mercy to all the worlds, and upon his virtuous family; and be pleased with his chosen companions. Make us of those who are most beloved to him and his family, and make our love for him and his family the most of all people. And make us leaders of the God conscious. Through us, elevate the truth and the banner of faith. Make our enemies Your enemies, and support us over them by your mercy, O Most Merciful.

---

[17] Sunan Ad-Darimi.

14

The Accusation of Sabotaging
the Date Harvesting Season

It is cited in Sahih Muslim, *related by Aisha and Thabit and Anas,* that 'the Messenger (PBUH) passed by a group [of farmers] cross-pollinating [date palm trees], and thus he said to them: "If you abstain from doing this, it would still produce (dates)." However, the dates came out spoiled. Thereafter, he passed by them once again and asked, "what is with your dates?" They replied: "You told us to do such and such," he responded by saying: "You are more aware of your worldly affairs [than me]."'[1]

It is certainly the case that not a single child from the children of Medina was unaware of the process of cross-pollination of date palm trees, so how is it conceivable that the one who is sent as the teacher would be ignorant regarding it, let alone being the most superior in knowledge and wisdom even before the revelation began? In fact, the Messenger (PBUH) detailed the creation of the date palm tree itself, stating, '[The date palm tree] is created from the remainder of the clay used to create Adam (AS).'[2]

---

1   Sahih Muslim.
2   Al-Qurtubi.

Did the Messenger manage poorly the worldly life? Such a stance squanders one's actions that can lead to benefit in the hereafter. Allah (SWT) says, 'Do not forget your portion in this world' (28:77). Thus, there is no meaning to the Hadith except to negate knowledge for the Messenger (PBUH) or to affirm upon him insufficient knowledge regarding the worldly life and attribute it to another person!

There are two stances regarding this matter. Some (scholars) say that the lack of knowledge of the Messenger is in that which is other than revelation. This stance is forwarded by those who consider that he erred in choosing the correct position for his troops in the Battle of Badr and thereafter was corrected by one of his companions who offered a more suitable alternative. However, this position is refuted by the fact that the Messenger was fully aware where each enemy would fall in the battlefield, and he was proved true. As this designation was made before the beginning of the Battle, then how can the one who knows the exact place of death of the enemy be lacking in planning for the position of his army?

However, other scholars say that the Messenger has a lack of knowledge regarding all aspects, including matters of revelation. This stance is forwarded by those who accept the implications of the ahadith of the captives of Badr, which claim that he acted in opposition to the revelation until Umar corrected him and that revelation came thereafter to confirm the stance of Umar![3] This stance is further promoted by those who confirm the Hadith regarding Ibn Salul and the Messenger's prayer upon him, insinuating that he is on occasion not the most knowledgeable of men and that he interferes in the affairs of the farmers of Medina without knowledge and sabotages their yields!

This is how the Messenger (PBUH) is depicted! He enters the affairs of people without knowledge and proposes destructive legal opinions that are detrimental to the economy of the city! Are we to hold true what they presume, that the Messenger (PBUH) has no knowledge of agriculture? Was he not the most intelligent of creation? Is it not that

---

[3]   See Chapter 1.

even a child from the children of Medina was aware of the process of cross-pollination of date palm trees? Is it not from sound intellect that one should not delve into a matter without knowledge? How is it possible then that the Messenger (PBUH) lacks such an intellect?

15

The Accusation of Gluttony

It is recorded in the Sunan of ad-Darimi:

> Abu Ubaid cooked (a lamb) for the Prophet (PBUH) in a cooking pot. The Prophet said to him, 'give me the shoulder,' since he used to enjoy the shoulder. He gave him the shoulder. The Prophet then said, 'Give me the shoulder.' Thus, he again gave him a shoulder. The Prophet (PBUH) again said: 'Give me the shoulder', Abu Ubaid replied, 'Oh Messenger of God, how many shoulders does a lamb have?' He said: 'By Him in whose Hand my soul resides, had you complied, you would have given me as many shoulders as I requested.'[1]

The obvious question in response to this Hadith is, would the Prophet (PBUH) eat shoulder (meat) ad infinitum? Yet it was the Messenger who would tie his stomach with stones and say 'it is sufficient for the son of Adam to eat enough to keep his back straight'! Hence, it is reported in at-Tirmidhi: 'There is no vessel that a person fills more evil than his stomach. It is sufficient for the son of Adam to eat enough to

---

[1]   Sunan ad-Darimi.

keep his back straight, and if this is not possible: then a third for food, a third for drink and a third for breathing.'[2]

As a consequence, the depiction of the Messenger (PBUH) in their eyes is that of a man who sits next to a cooking pot that's already on the stove and eats from it whilst it is on the fire and doesn't wait for the food to be served. What is more, his requests for seconds never cease! Is this the depiction of the crowning creation of Allah (SWT)? Is this how the Messenger (PBUH) is regarded?

Today they will not attribute this type of depiction to a hungry Arab. If this type of ascription was made, depicting one of the heads or officials of an Arab nation, that he or she remains at a cooking pot and orders the chef to take out the meat and feed them the shoulder to no end, it would be grounds for severing ties between nations, if not of war! But when it comes to the beloved of Allah (SWT), for them it's easy to accept!

---

[2] Sunan at-Tirmidhi.

16

The Accusation of Forgetting the Qur'an

It is cited in Sahih al-Bukhari that Aisha said: 'Then the Messenger (PBUH) heard a man recite a chapter of the Qur'an at night, and said: "May God have mercy on him, indeed, he has reminded me of such and such a verse, that I had forgotten from such and such a chapter."'[1]

Allah (SWT) states in the Qur'an: 'We will make you recite [Oh Prophet], and you shall never forget' (87:6). That means, that which he recites will not be forgotten. If Allah (SWT) wants His Prophet (PBUH) to forget a verse, then it is inconceivable that another would be able to recall it to remind him! The Hadith does not mention the name of the person who recited; neither do the verses nor the chapter to which the 'forgotten' verses belong. In this case, did the narrator of the Hadith, who attributes forgetfulness to the Prophet (PBUH), forget the verses likewise? And did he also forget the man who recited these verses? Certainly, a man who reminds the Prophet (PBUH) of verses he had forgotten should be known and cannot be left nameless and unidentified. Thus, the affair is of utmost importance since it's related to the message, its fulfilment, and the means by which it is fulfilled!

---

[1] Sahih al-Bukhari.

How can a Muslim swallow the idea that the Messenger (PBUH) had forgotten what he was sent with? Truly, this is doubting the preservation of the Qur'an by Allah (SWT) and, furthermore, is accusing the Prophet (PBUH) of mislaying his message when Allah (SWT) says, 'Indeed, it is We who sent down the Dhikr (Qur'an) and indeed, We are its protector' (15:9).

Allah (SWT) also intimates to his beloved Messenger (PBUH), '(Oh Prophet), Move not your tongue with it [Qur'an], to hasten its recitation. Indeed, upon Us is its collection [in your heart] and its recitation [by your tongue]' (75:16–17), yet it is found in Bukhari, on the authority of Aisha (RA), that the Prophet (PBUH) had forgotten verses of his Qur'an and had to be reminded by another!

From Allah we are, and to Him we return.

17

The Accusation of Becoming Delirious

Are there amongst the Muslim scholars those who believe in the possibility of there being one who is superior to the Prophet (PBUH), whether it be in knowledge, awareness (of Allah), religion, or character? Is there one whom Allah (SWT) would support in favour of the Prophet (PBUH), whose actions He would prefer, and on whom He would grant approval above the Prophet (PBUH) if they differed? Would Allah (SWT) discipline His Prophet (PBUH) if he refused to accept the opinion of one of his companions? Is there truth to the statement that one of the senior companions disobeyed the Prophet deliberately in his presence and forbade the companions to carry out his commands and that despite this, people obeyed this companion? And is it appropriate for a companion to accuse the Prophet of diminished mental capacity and describe him as unfit in his presence?

No Muslim would deny that the Prophet (PBUH)—whether compared to the prophets and messengers of the past or from humanity at large—is the most knowledgeable, the most honourable, the dearest, and the most favoured in the sight of Allah (SWT). He is the sole legislator of his message (PBUH). This is the sound creed incumbent upon every Muslim. However, is this corroborated in the books of Sunnah that have reached us?

What would be your response, O Muslim, if it is said to you that the Prophet (PBUH) himself commanded those in his presence to carry out a task yet one from amongst them objected the command of the Prophet (PBUH) and instructed those present not to carry it out or respond to the Messenger (PBUH) since he has fallen ill, pain has overtaken him, and he has become delirious and that they are not in need of this command so long as they have the book of Allah (SWT)? Does this not mean disobedience and violation of this statement of Allah (SWT): 'Oh you who believe, respond to Allah and to the Messenger when he calls you to that which revitalises you' (8:24)? Can such a scenario be found in the books of Sunnah? If so, are they authentic? Are there Muslims that would say that this scenario is indeed found in the books of Sunnah, that they are authentic and not fabricated? Do such people believe it is possible to defy the Prophet, to accuse him in his presence of diminished mental capacity, and to say that since he was overtaken by pain and had become delirious, his statements should not be taken seriously?

Are the likes of these statements acceptable from a respected companion who loves the Prophet (PBUH) and obeys Allah (SWT) in accordance with His words: 'Let those who contravene the Prophet's order be warned' (24:63)? Would these types of statements emanate from one who believes in the infallibility of the Prophet (PBUH) as confirmed by Allah (SWT): 'Your companion has not strayed, nor has he erred. Nor does he speak with any inclination. It is only revelation, revealed to him' (53:3–5)? Would someone who believes in the infallibility of the Prophet say such things? Does illness affect the Prophet's mental state that it would necessitate abandoning what he says? This means that such a person questions the soundness of the Prophet's (PBUH) mental ability!

How would one who issues forth such a repulsive claim know that an illness has indeed affected the mind of the Prophet? Did Allah (SWT) make manifest the interior of His Prophet (PBUH) and the status of his mind to such a person so that it became known to him that he was delirious from illness, speaking beside himself due to being overtaken by pain and therefore dismantling the message that he was sent with from Allah (SWT) and changing the words of Allah (SWT) and His message due to being overwhelmed by illness to the point of delirium?

The perpetration of these acts—namely, forbidding those present from obeying the Prophet's order and treating him as being delirious and out of his mind—is attributed to Umar bin al-Khattab!

It is cited in Sahih al-Bukhari that Ibn Abbas said, 'When the pain of the Prophet (PBUH) intensified, he said: "Bring me a sheet [for writing], so that I can dictate for you a will that would save you from ever going astray." Umar responded: "Indeed, the Prophet (PBUH) has been overcome by pain, and we have the book of Allah, it is enough for us." Disagreement followed and clamour heightened. The Prophet (PBUH) said: "Leave me, dispute in my presence is not acceptable." Ibn Abbas (RA) left repeating: "What a calamity, an absolute calamity, that which prevented the Messenger from (writing) his will."[1] And this is from the narration of Muslims: 'The Prophet (PBUH) said: "Bring me shoulder bone and an ink-pot, or a plate and some ink, so that I can dictate for you a will that would save you from ever going astray." They responded: "Indeed, the Prophet is delirious."'[2]

If Umar refused to bring forth a tablet and an inkpot and forbade those present to do likewise on the grounds that the Prophet (PBUH) had been overcome by his illness and is delirious, then why did Umar not reject the order of the Prophet, 'Leave me be, it is not befitting that you argue in my presence,' on the same grounds of the previous command and then refuse to leave him?

The statement 'Indeed, the Prophet (PBUH) has been overcome by pain, and you have the Holy Qur'an, the book of Allah is enough for us' calls into question the dictates of the Prophet to the extent of denying his wishes in the guiding of the umma![3]

---

[1]   Sahih al-Bukhari.
[2]   Sahih Muslim.
[3]   The Muslim community.

Indeed, it is objection to his wishes specifically related to his message, the guidance of the umma from misguidance, which befits none other than the Prophet himself, as Allah (SWT) says, 'So they should not contend with you over this matter' (22:67). He remains a Prophet and a Messenger despite his illness until he meets Allah (SWT), and it is compulsory upon every Muslim to obey him and his commands since it is akin to obeying Allah (SWT). How could disobedience and refusal to observe his commands take place at the hands of the Muslims? Allah (SWT) says, 'He does not speak with any inclination. It is only revelation, revealed to him' (53:3–4). And there is this holy verse: 'And whatever the Messenger consigns unto you, take it, and from whatever he forbids you, abstain' (59:7). How can they deem contravening his words to be the appropriate position? Is it a position of concern regarding what he is going say, or is it an accusation of his mental state? Or perhaps he may corrupt what is mentioned in the book of Allah (SWT) or to establish that which opposes it?

Can all this be rightly attributed to Umar (RA)? He said, 'We have the book of Allah, it is enough for us,' yet the book of Allah (SWT) obligates Muslims to willingly accept the Messenger's dictates. 'And whatever the Messenger consigns unto you, take it' (59:7)! This position depicts the Prophet (PBUH) as someone whose statements, during his illness, cannot be given credence to, his Prophethood having been terminated and his infallibility no longer applicable as if he has become a normal human being who is ill, demoting the necessity of accepting his commands! Furthermore, the dictates of another person have become superior to the statements of the Prophet and his orders!

Thus, if we give credence to this Hadith, refuse to accept it as fabricated, and believe the authenticity of its attribution to Umar, then what is left of his Islam? Opposition to the Prophet (PBUH), refusal of his dictates, and accusation of his mental state invalidate one's Islam. In this case, the Prophet (PBUH) commanded for the bringing of a tablet and an inkpot, whilst Umar opposed him and ordered to not bring the tablet and an inkpot! If it is claimed that Umar is justified in what he said, then to whom belongs the support of Allah, necessitating obedience and precluding defiance?

18

The Accusation of Dread at the Deathbed

It is related in Sahih al-Bukhari, on the authority of Aisha (RA), the wife of the Prophet (PBUH), who said:

> When the illness of the messenger (PBUH) worsened and his pain grew severe, he requested that he be nursed in my house. The wives concurred. Thus, the Prophet arrived supported by two men, and his legs were dragging on the ground, between Abbas, and another man. Ubaid-Ullah said, 'I informed Abdullah bin Abbas of what Aisha said. Ibn Abbas said: 'Do you know who the other man was?' I replied in the negative. Ibn Abbas said, 'He was Ali.'[1] Aisha further said, 'When the Prophet arrived at my house and his pain grew severe, he ordered us to pour over him, seven skins full of water, so that he may give advice to the people. So he was seated in a Mikhdab[2] belonging to Hafsa, the wife of the Prophet. Thereafter, we all started pouring water over him from the water skins till he beckoned us to stop. Subsequently, he went out to the people, led them in prayer and addressed them.'[3]

---

[1] The cousin and son-in-law of the Prophet.

[2] A vessel in which clothes are washed.

[3] Sahih al-Bukhari.

A statement that is also attributed to the messenger (PBUH) during such a time is 'Oh my fears'![4] This tells of his dread at the deathbed! Does this mean that the Prophet (PBUH) feared coming to an evil end? Did he not permit the angel of death to enter? Did he not love to meet Allah (SWT)? Is it praise to mention the dread of a person upon death? Is there anyone who is more fearless and brave than the messenger of Allah (PBUH)? Moreover, the water of seven untied skins is not sufficient to fill the entire room!

---

4   It is stated in the Kamil of Ibn al-Athir: 'The messenger scooped water between his noble hands and washed his face saying; "oh my fears", whereupon Fatima (AS) replied: "I fear due to your fears, oh father", upon which the Messenger said: "there will be no fear upon your father after this day."'

19

The Accusation of Lacking Authority
in the Divine Message

If we have faith in Allah (SWT), it follows that we give credence to the Messenger of Allah (PBUH) that he is sent by his Lord. This stance attests to the conviction that the Messenger received a revelation, the eternal words of Allah, which is protected from all falsehood. We find that Allah (SWT) has referred us in His book to the Messenger (PBUH): 'And whatever the Messenger consigns unto you, take it, and from whatever he forbids you, abstain' (59:7). Notice that Allah (SWT) doesn't say 'Whatever I consign unto you, take it' just as He mentions 'Let those who contravene the Prophet's order be warned, lest tribulation strike them or a painful punishment' (24:63), making tribulations, misfortune, and punishment a consequence of disobeying the Messenger since obeying him is akin to obeying Allah (SWT). 'He who obeys the Messenger has indeed obeyed Allah' (4:80).

As a result, the entire umma is referred by Allah (SWT) to the Messenger (PBUH), to submit to him, follow, obey, and take from him, and by obligation, not to disobey him since disobedience to him is disobedience to Allah (SWT). Consequently, absolute authority for the Muslims is the Messenger of Allah (PBUH) in the present life, just as in the hereafter, since He (SWT) has appointed him to such a position with exclusion of the other messengers. It is in him where the affairs of creation is concluded since he intercedes for them by his exclusive intercession in the presence of Allah (SWT) to judge between them. Similarly, the affair of the major sinners amongst his umma is concluded by him by his special intercession, separating them from the fire and gaining entry to paradise.

Thus, Allah (SWT) has elevated his mention in the present life and the hereafter. 'And We have raised high for you your mention' (94:4). And Allah (SWT) promised to accept all those who come to Him (Glory be to Him) through the path of the Prophet (PBUH) in this life and the hereafter. He is the utmost beloved, the preceding seal, whose affairs are the affairs of Allah (SWT), whose throwing[1] is the throwing of Allah, whose speech is the speech of Allah (SWT). 'He does not speak with any inclination. It is only revelation, revealed to him' (53:03–4).

Indeed, He (SWT) took the covenant of the prophets to believe in the Messenger (PBUH) and support him. 'And when Allah took the covenant of the Prophets (saying) "Behold that which I have given you of the Scripture and wisdom and then there comes to you a Messenger confirming what is with you, you have to believe in him and support him." He [Allah then] said: "Have you acknowledged and assumed My covenant?" They replied, "We have acknowledged it." He said: "Then bear witness, and I am with you among the witnesses"' (3:81). Furthermore, He (SWT) commanded the believers to honour him, support him, and exalt him. 'That you believe in Allah and His Messenger, honour him, respect him and exalt him morning and evening' (48:9).

It is astounding that, after all the above, it is still considered legitimate by many daring to talk about him to criticise and lessen the upstanding status of his character, his knowledge, and his actions! This position can only be maintained by those who regard themselves as more complete in knowledge than him and who claim the ability of receiving this knowledge directly from Allah (SWT) so as to confirm what they say about him. Thus, they attribute to the

---

[1]   See verse 7:17.

Messenger (PBUH) frowning in the face of a blind man[2] though he was sent to perfect moral character! They describe him as lacking knowledge regarding the worldly life though he was sent as a teacher! They characterise him as being deficient in planning for the position of his army during the Battle of Badr, though he was fully aware where each enemy would fall in the battlefield and was proved true! This designation was made before the beginning of the battle, so how then can the one who knows the exact place of death of the enemy be deficient in planning for the position of his army? May my soul, my children, my parents be sacrificed for your sake, O Messenger of Allah (SWT); no umma has disparaged their Prophet as your umma has disparaged you.

It is alleged that authority is to the Qur'an. This claim promotes the notion that the alleger is in fact the authority or at least the commentator[3] to whom one refers regarding it. It is inconceivable for one to be the authority of the Qur'an since the Qur'an assigns authority to the Messenger (PBUH). 'And whatever the Messenger consigns unto you, take it, and from whatever he forbids you, abstain' (59:7). Thus, whoever promotes this stance wishes to withdraw authority from the Messenger (PBUH) and place it upon those who claim it, the false claimers of knowledge and the Qur'an interpretation.

The Qur'an is interpreted by the human being to the extent of his intellect, and one will fall short in penetrating the Qur'an no matter how much one struggles, interprets, and analyses since it is the words of Allah (SWT). Its wonders are infinite, its marvels are immeasurable, and the total knowledge of it is unattainable. Those who maintain this position are unaware of this statement of Allah (SWT): 'And We revealed to you (oh Muhammad) the Dhikr (knowledge) so that you clarify to the people what was sent down to them and that they might contemplate,' (16:44). They have placed themselves in the position of the Prophet so that it may be they who make clear to the people what was sent down of the Qur'an!

---

2   See Chapter 6.
3   Commentators of the Qur'an.

All those who undertake Qur'anic enquiry are in need of the Messenger (PBUH), the teacher, for clarification. Indeed, Allah (SWT) says, 'Bow and prostrate yourselves' (22:77). This is a clear command of bowing and prostrating, in explicit language, and therefore one feels it may not require clarification and interpretation from the teacher (PBUH). Yet when the Prophet (PBUH) clarified the verse, he rose from the bowing position until he became upright and then descended to the position of prostration. Hence, it is inappropriate for anyone to have the audacity to attribute authority to the Qur'an and to apply its rulings without recourse to the Messenger and then, with this limited understanding, insolently adjudicate the Messenger's actions, knowledge, and behaviour with that which is unbefitting his perfection!

It is arrogated by those who are ignorant and undirected that the Prophet (PBUH) is a human being like other human beings due to their understanding of this verse: 'Say, "I am only a human like you (plural)"' (17:110). This is due to a constrained intellect; concern is not given to this statement of the Messenger (PBUH): 'Indeed, I am unlike any one of you. It is my Lord who feeds me and quenches my thirst'!⁴ Had these odious fatwas, which repudiate the infallibility of the Prophet (PBUH), not been hastened and stubbornly insisted upon, they would have come to the realisation that the Prophet (PBUH), unlike any one of them, was void of shadow.

He was able to see from his rear equally as his fore. His eyes slept whilst his heart remained vigilant. The tree responded to his call, drawing near to him and leaving the ground fissured. He asked the lizard of who he was, and it testified to his Message. Stones greeted him, and camels aired their grievances to him. The stem of the tree stump sobbed due to his adoption of an alternative place for minbar,⁵ which only ceased after he caressed it with his blessed hands. He

---

4   Musnad Ahmad.
5   Ceremony pulpit.

(PBUH) promised Suraqah[6] the bracelets of Khosrau,[7] which came
to pass after more than twenty years; this meant that the Prophet
(PBUH) was aware of Suraqah's age and that he would live to see the
downfall of Khosrau along with the bracelets passing on to him!

How great is his knowledge! And how great a teacher! Regrettably, his
own community is unaware of him, and he has been disparaged unlike
any other Prophet! Each mufassir who claims that authority is to the
Qur'an in fact yields to their own interpretations, which culminate
in the limits of his knowledge and understanding. Such scholars are
unable to exceed their own selves—that is, their understanding of
the Qur'an—and this becomes their reference and ultimate authority,
believing authority to be from the Qur'an itself! Hence, each scholar,
or ideologue, in and of themselves become an independent authority,
presuming they have a say as to the infallibility of the Messenger from
their understanding, leading to a multiplicity of authorities, equalling
the multiplicity of scholars and ideologues!

Thus, agreement amongst 'those who believe' was never reached,
and their schools of thought in the religion multiplied, just as views
regarding the Messenger (PBUH) multiplied. And their perceptions
diversified regarding his relationship to his Lord. He became the target
of their criticism regarding his knowledge, presupposing it, instead of
being one whom they are devoted to, from whom they take knowledge
just as a student from a teacher since he was sent a teacher for all
mankind, the leader of the children of Adam, the one who possesses
the indispensable knowledge of the world, and the intercession in the
hereafter.

Moreover, he became the subject of differences of opinions, and his
status and infallibility were questioned, not to mention his stances
being compared to those who are ordinary amongst his followers and
umma! Consequently, it is deemed that he erred in opinion regarding

---

[6]   A companion who concealed the news about the Prophet after the
bounty that was put upon the capture or killing of him (PBUH) during
his emigration to Medina.

[7]   The Persian king at the time.

the story of the POWs of Badr, whilst another proved correct. It is deemed that he erred in his conduct in delivering the message of perfect moral character, which he was sent with, and received a poor blind man with contempt and frowned in his face, ultimately depicting him as one who acted in contrary to his message!

Their belief is such due to the notion that the ahadith proposes it, as in that found in Musnad Ahmed: 'Abu Hurayra said: "Then the Prophet became delirious [i.e. he spoke with words that had no meaning]. I prayed, and sat next to him, he said to me: 'Ashkunb darad' I responded by saying, 'no oh Messenger of Allah,' to that he said: 'Pray, since in prayer there is cure.'"[8] The statement 'Ashkunb[9] darad' is as a form of madness, which Abu Hurayra is attempting to attribute to the Messenger (PBUH) since his hastened response was no. Thus the Prophet (PBUH) said to him, 'Pray.' And yet he had already prayed before he sat next to the Messenger, portraying the Messenger as being delirious whilst Abu Hurayra prays! If Abu Hurayra truly stated this Hadith, then it is only he who was delirious, unbalanced, and hallucinating, not the infallible Prophet (PBUH), who speaks not from his own desires.[10]

Thus, the portrait that they paint is of one who speaks nonsense at times due to delirium and insanity. Thereupon, how can they consider him infallible, that he speaks not from his own desires, and that taking from him and abstaining from his forbiddances is incumbent? Allah (SWT) says, 'When the wrongdoers say, "You follow not but a man bewitched"' (17:47). This is the semblance portrayed. Whilst a companion is in connection with Allah (SWT) through prayer, the Messenger reclines, speaking nonsense! What a difference between the one who is delirious and the one who stands in prayer in the presence of Allah (SWT)!

Allah (SWT) states, 'See what similitudes they coin for you; so they have gone astray, and cannot find a way' (17:48). Is this the condition

---

8   Musnad Ahmed.

9   *Ashkunba* has no meaning in the Arabic language.

10   See verse 53:3.

of the Messenger and the state of Abu Hurayra? This depiction is disgraceful, except for those who wish to mock our religion and sacred matters.

Allah (SWT), in the noble Qur'an, has referred the Muslim umma in its entirety to the Prophet (PBUH), to take from him. He made it compulsory to follow him and cautioned against disobeying him. Therefore, he is the standard reference as mentioned. If such is the case, then it is mandatory to remove those ahadith that posit others in his place, yield to them knowledge above his knowledge, or afford them Sunnah equal to his Sunnah. It is from the incompetence of the intellect, if not manifest disbelief, that they accept these ahadith that place others from his umma—companion or not—in instances of superiority regarding affairs of religion or the guidance of the umma. Regarding all things relating to the Messenger, it is obligatory to behold them through the prism of learning and receive them through the comportment of tutelage over and above any scholar or faqih[11] or lover and every Muslim and not through the eye of criticism, leading oneself to utter inequities regarding his infallibility due to dependence upon one's intellect as the authority and reference source. In reality, such perpetrators find no reference or authority except to Bukhari and Muslim and other ahadith literature, including accounts of *sirah* and Qur'anic commentaries, which they use to condemn the Messenger (PBUH)!

It may be remarked that if so, then from where does one research or speak about the Prophet (PBUH) if not from these sources of religion that have become sacrosanct amongst the Muslims? I confirm that these have enormous merit in recollecting the life of the Prophet (PBUH), including his sayings and historical accounts; however, they cannot be afforded infallibility since this only applies to the Prophet (PBUH). If one accepts fully their contents—including those that contravene the infallibility of the Prophet—it indeed affords infallibility to these texts!

---

[11]   Scholar of jurisprudence.

It may also be enquired, how does one determine which of those to accept and reject? We respond: all Hadith text that is found diminishing the status of the Messenger (PBUH)—the ultimate authority—or depositing another in his place or raising another above his status in certain circumstances or preferring this person above him in matters of religion must be ruled out, disqualified, and rejected. At the same time, hold on to the noble status of the beloved, whom every Muslim should have faith in, believing that his status cannot truly be fathomed by the human intellect since he is the ultimate authority!

He is beyond all of creation in rank, knowledge, and status in the sight of Allah (SWT) and the true believers, and his companions are simply one product of his virtue. It is beyond the realms of possibility that one of them can equal him, let alone be superior to him (PBUH)! Indeed, such a notion is sacrilegious and hurting to whom it is attributed, especially if that one is aware of the status of the Messenger of Allah (PBUH) in view of his Lord and loves him more than himself.[12]

The detractor places himself in all situations in the rank of the teacher and authority and not of an acquiring student. Thus, each and every detractor of the Messenger (PBUH) has indeed placed himself upon the position of a teacher in the religion and placed the Prophet (PBUH) in a place of criticism, thereby lowering his status below that of himself so as to criticise him! He who puts himself in this position has indeed reached such a level of arrogance, placing himself above the Prophet, which excommunicates him from Islam!

---

[12] See Hadith of love.

20

Epilogue

The previous chapters are not exhaustive to say the least regarding what is authorised within the sources of Islam: the true message brought by the greatest creation of Allah (SWT), the noblest of the messengers, and the Seal of the Prophets, confirming the truth of the books before him—the Torah and the Bible.[1] He was sent to perfect moral character that was brought by all the previous messengers. He is the certifier of their message and the clarifier of what their followers differed over. 'And We have not revealed to you the Book [Oh Muhammad], except for you to clarify for them what they differed over, and as guidance' (16:64).

Thus, what has been mentioned represents a small sample of what is overflowing within what is called the sources and references of Islam; however, they claimed, unjustly and falsely, that these are the most authentic books after the book of Allah (SWT). As a result, they have become fully accepted by those bereft of intellectual critique and purified hearts, admitting that which is inadmissible for the Messenger (PBUH), whom Allah (SWT) venerated, ennobled, and prayed upon along with his angels. Allah commanded the believers to send prayers upon him and obligated obedience to and reverence of him.

---

[1]   See verse 3:2.

This is the true obedience to Allah (SWT) and His command upon His servants: 'And whoever deviates from Our command—We will make him taste the punishment of the Flames' (42:12). And this is on the day when there will remain no refuge save for the mercy of Allah (SWT), the Messenger (PBUH). Thus, whoever arrives on the Day of Judgement critical of the Messenger (PBUH) will arrive despairing of the mercy of Allah (SWT).

He who absolves his intellect for another and gives credence to everything that is found in these sources and ignorantly issues judgement upon Allah (SWT)—that he limits his grace to the predecessors[2] and that there remains none for those who come after—will be grovelling on his face[3] since he unashamedly finds no objection to what is attributed to the Messenger (PBUH), which even an ordinary Muslim would not attribute to himself.

He who holds such an assumption is bereft of shame, and the Hadith mentions: 'Indeed among that which reached the people from the words of the earlier prophethood: "if you lack shame, then do whatever you wish."'[4] Therefore, such a person sees no offence in the malicious accusations levelled against the Messenger (PBUH). What is more, he perceives it to be knowledge, as it's present in the sources of Islam, so he keeps on propagating it on the pulpits. Due to this, those who are ignorant and simple-minded—many of those called to Islam included—accept such attributions due to the frequency of their reiteration without studying the sources or taking it from a teacher, and then they speak about the city of knowledge, the master of the children of Adam critically!

These nineteen accusations are not exclusive in the sources of Islam but rather are a clarification for him who desires to take heed or desires to be thankful[5] and a refinement for his heart. I hope that they will be a warning for the negligent, illumination for the scholar,

---

2   The predecessors (*salaf*) are the first two generations of Muslims.
3   See verse 67:22.
4   Sahih al-Bukhari.
5   See verse 25:62.

enlightenment for the lover, and salvation for the Muslims from the abyss of hell that spares nothing and leaves nothing intact,[6] as over it are nineteen keepers.[7]

Likewise, nineteen totals the number of letters that compose the *basmala*,[8] the protector of ills if recited at the beginning of an action, whilst being devoid of it renders the action cut short, severed, and defective. Nineteen also totals the number of letters that compose the *hasbala*,[9] which protects from evil its reciter by the grace of Allah (SWT). And to Allah (SWT) is the final destination, from him is aid sought, and to him is trust placed.

All praise is due to Allah (SWT), first and last, and thanks to the Messenger of Allah, the kind, the merciful,[10] in the beginning and in the end. O Allah (SWT), send prayers and blessings upon Muhammad, his parents, and his family.

---

[6]   See verse 74:28.

[7]   See verse 74:30.

[8]   The name given to the recurring Islamic phrase 'In the name of God, the most gracious, the most merciful'.

[9]   The supplication meaning 'Allah is sufficient for us and the best disposer of affairs'.

[10] See verse 9:128.

Publications by the Author

1. *Holistic Nature of the Human Being* (Arabic): published by the Arab Establishment for Research and Publication, 2012.
2. *The All-Embracing Message of Islam* (English): published by Outskirts Press, Inc., 2009.
3. *Revisions of Islamic Thought* (volume 1, Arabic): published by Ward Jordanian House for Publishing and Distribution 2008.
4. *Revisions of Islamic Thought* (volumes 1 and 2, Arabic): published by the Arab Establishment for Research and Publication, 2014.
5. *Islam and the State* (Arabic): published by the Arab Establishment for Research and Publication, first edition in 2011 and second edition in 2015.
6. *A Prophet from the Land of Sudan* (Arabic): published by the Arab Establishment for Research and Publication, 2011.
7. *Having Faith in Muhammad* (Arabic): published by the Arab Establishment for Research and Publication, 2012.
8. *The Remedy of Souls from Accusations Held by Muslims Against the Prophet* (Arabic): published by the Arab Establishment for Research and Publication, 2013.
9. *The Bright Lights of Love* (poetry, Arabic): published by the Arab Establishment for Research and Publication, 2014.
10. *Accusations of the Master of God's Messengers by Qur'an Interpreters* (Arabic): published by the Arab Establishment for Research and Publication, 2016.

About the Author

Sheikh Elnayyal Abu Groon, descendent of Prophet Muhammad (PBUH), was born in Sudan in 1947 in Abu Groon, the home of the Sufi traditional institution of his renowned grandfather, Sheikh Muhammad Abu Groon. His father, Sheikh Abdel Qadir, was a unique reformer of virtues upon the footsteps of Prophet Muhammad (PBUH). He raised his son upon loving Prophet Muhammad (PBUH) and living pure Islam. He graduated with a degree in law from the University of Khartoum in 1970 and has been high court judge and legal affairs minister.

In the early 1970s, the author wrote his first book, *Al-Sirat al-Mustaqeem* ('The straight path'), a brief but comprehensive account on Islamic theology. Since then, the author has completed a series of books on revision of Islamic thought and heritage, using his own unprecedented rigorous methodology of research. This included criteria for checking the authenticity of prophetic traditions (Sunnah) and the accuracy of Qur'anic interpretations since they constitute the basis for Islamic heritage. This methodology is outlined in the introductory section of this book.

Short descriptions of selected works of the author include:

Islam and the State (Arabic): The author challenges all political theories and movements that advocate Islam as a system of governance. Utilising textual evidence, the author argues that Islam is the religion sent from God, devoid of compulsion ('There is no compulsion in religion'), whilst a state is a political system of governance imposed by law.

Accusations of the Master of God's Messengers by Qur'an Interpreters (Arabic): The author presents a comprehensive methodology of understanding the holy Qur'an. Through critical analysis from interpretations of leading exegetes, the author exposes a number of serious accusations levelled at the Prophet (PBUH).